AUSTRALIANS
THE GUIDE AND INDEX

*'You are invaders of their country' was the headline that
accompanied this illustration by David Bromley with a book
review of Henry Reynold's* Frontier *(1987), published by
Allen & Unwin.* Sydney Morning Herald,
25 April 1987.

JOHN FAIRFAX & SONS

AUSTRALIANS
THE GUIDE AND INDEX

FAIRFAX, SYME & WELDON ASSOCIATES

AUSTRALIANS: A HISTORICAL LIBRARY
AUSTRALIANS: THE GUIDE AND INDEX

First published 1987 by
Fairfax, Syme & Weldon Associates
235 Jones Street, Broadway
New South Wales 2007, Australia

Publishing Director
Kevin Weldon

Editorial Director
Elaine Russell

Managing Editor
Kim Anderson

Indexer
Elmar Zalums

Consultant Indexer
Jean Haggar

Secretary
Monica Stuardo

Editors
Sheena Coupe
Claire Craig
Margo Lanagan

Art Director
John Bull
Bull's Graphics

Designer
Diana Wells

Production Manager
Mick Bagnato

© Copyright Fairfax, Syme & Weldon Associates 1987

National Library of Australia
Cataloguing-in-Publication Data

Australians: a historical library
Includes bibliographies and index.
ISBN 0 949288 09 8 (set).
ISBN 0 949288 18 7 (set : deluxe).
ISBN 0 949288 31 4 (The guide and index).
ISBN 0 949288 32 2 (The guide and index : deluxe).

1. Australia – History. I. Title: Australians to 1788.
II. Title: Australians 1838. III. Title: Australians
1888. IV. Title: Australians 1938. V. Title: Australians
from 1939. VI. Title: Australians, a historical atlas.
VII. Title: Australians, a guide to sources. VIII.
Title: Australians, events and places. IX. Title:
Australians, a historical dictionary. X. Title:
Australians, historical statistics.

994

Typeset and Printed at Griffin Press, Netley, South Australia 5037, Australia.

Fairfax, Syme & Weldon Associates is a partnership between John Fairfax & Sons Limited, David Syme & Co. Limited and Kevin Weldon & Associates Pty Ltd.

Published outside Australia by Cambridge University Press
The Pitt Building, Trumpington Street, Cambridge CB2 1RP 32 East 57th Street, New York, NY 10022, USA
ISBN 0 521 34073 X (set, Cambridge University Press).

COVER ILLUSTRATION
'Bondi' poster by Percy Trompf.
Courtesy of the estate of Percy Trompf.

FOREWORD

Australians: A Historical Library has been ten years in the making. Published by Fairfax, Syme & Weldon Associates, it is the product of a partnership formed in 1982 between John Fairfax & Sons Limited, David Syme & Co Limited and Kevin Weldon & Associates Pty Limited. This partnership has brought together the strengths and skills of Australia's pre-eminent publishers of quality newspapers and its most entrepreneurial publisher, Kevin Weldon, with his long experience in the production and marketing of quality books.

The idea for the project originated with a group of Australia's most respected historians who wanted to commemorate the Bicentenary of European settlement in Australia with a multivolume history of the continent. It soon became evident, however, that the major publishing houses of Australia, including those with strong international affiliations, would be unlikely to undertake this large venture because of the uncertain market prospects and the high investment required. John Paton, who was then Group Marketing Manager of David Syme & Co Limited, initiated discussions with members (in particular Ken Inglis) of the Management Committee of History Project Incorporated, as the authors eventually became known, and the managements of the three companies who were to form the partnership. In our discussions we sought a workable approach to the financing, production and marketing of what was to become Australia's largest book publishing venture.

The scale of the project created a need for enormous funding and the publishers received no direct grants from State and Commonwealth governments, or the Australian Bicentennial Authority. Moreover, they assisted the authors by royalty advances on a scale unprecedented in Australian publishing history. This financial support encouraged the authors to take a much bolder approach to the scope of both text and illustration than that originally envisaged. Fairfax, Syme & Weldon committed millions of dollars to the editing, production and printing of the books, and have also undertaken to donate to the Australian Bicentennial Authority a royalty of one per cent of the net receipts from the sale of the first edition to help the Authority fund its activities. The three companies in the partnership were prepared to invest in this enterprise without the prospect of normal commercial returns and *Australians: a historical library* is their contribution to the nation's Bicentenary.

The successful publication of *Australians: a historical library* is a tribute to the determination and dedication of many people. The efforts to achieve excellence in all aspects of editing, design and production, using Australian paper and printing, have been amply rewarded by the results, which have confirmed the soundness of the partnership's vision. The closely knit relationship between publishers and authors, working with many educational institutions, has been fundamental to the ultimate success of the project.

PHILIP ALLEN

JOHN FAIRFAX & SONS LIMITED

The Fairfax name has been a leading force in Australia's newspaper industry since 8 February 1841, when John Fairfax became co-owner of *The Sydney Herald* – known today as *The Sydney Morning Herald.*

On 31 December 1856, John Fairfax took his son, James Reading Fairfax, into partnership with himself and his eldest son Charles. They formed John Fairfax & Sons, which has provided the foundation and continuity for the company until the present time.

John Fairfax Limited was incorporated as a public company on 9 April 1956 with later generations of the family still holding a controlling interest. The Fairfax organisation then consisted of the holding company, John Fairfax Limited, and various subsidiary companies, notably John Fairfax & Sons Limited.

The flagship of the company, *The Sydney Morning Herald*, has been published continuously since April 1831 and has provided 156 years of reporting national and international news and events. Through its pages the history and development of our nation has been chronicled, from the fledgling colony to the sophisticated multicultural society of today.

The Sydney Morning Herald and the many other publications of the Fairfax organisation, have provided a seldom paralleled standard of journalistic excellence and impartiality throughout their long history. Few media organisations can claim such a heritage in the printed word or the recording of Australian history.

It is fitting, therefore, that John Fairfax & Sons Limited has played a major role in making possible the publishing of *Australians: a historical libarary.*

DAVID SYME & CO LIMITED

David Syme & Co Limited publish the Melbourne *Age*, widely regarded as one of the world's finest newspapers. From its first issue published on 17 October 1854, the opening day of Melbourne's first inter-colonial exhibition and the year in which Cobb & Co began their coach run between Melbourne and the goldmining town of Bendigo, *The Age* has endeavoured to record *great movements, the advocacy of free institutions, the diffusion of truth, and the advancement of man*. Throughout the years, *The Age* has remained independent of party and sectional interest, and has played a creative role in the development of Victoria and, indeed, the whole of Australia.

Ebenezer Syme purchased *The Age* in 1856. After his death in 1860 his brother, David Syme, published the paper, first on the family's behalf and then as the sole proprietor. For 38 years the story of *The Age* was largely the story of David Syme, and until the 1980s members of his family continued to play a major role in the company.

Ranald Macdonald, the Managing Director of the company in 1983, was a great grandson of David Syme, and he enthusiastically supported the formation of Fairfax, Syme & Weldon Associates to produce and market *Australians: a historical library*. In 1984, while working on this great publishing enterprise, the partnership, underwritten by David Syme & Co Limited, also successfully published *The Victorians*, a three volume history written for the sesquicentennial of the state.

The company also has a network of community newspapers in suburban Melbourne, and a range of consumer and business magazines. It also owns the *Warnambool Standard* and is associated with a number of regional and weekly newspapers.

KEVIN WELDON & ASSOCIATES PTY LTD

Kevin Weldon is the former founding managing director of the Hamlyn Group. In this role he was responsible for many successful publishing programs, including the *Australia's heritage* weekly series in the early 1970s, and *The greatest island*, one of the best selling books of the early 1980s.

In 1980, he formed Kevin Weldon & Associates Pty Ltd, followed in 1981 by The Macquarie Library Pty Ltd, created to publish Australia's national dictionary, the highly successful *Macquarie dictionary*, and other Macquarie titles, including the *Macquarie thesaurus* and *The Macquarie illustrated world atlas*.

In 1985, the Weldon–Hardie group was created with Kevin Weldon as chairman and chief executive. It includes the imprints of Lansdowne, Rigby, Ure Smith, Rigby Education, Intercontinental Publishing Corporation (the international division of the group), Weldons, *Geo* and *Nature & Health* magazines, as well as a direct mail division. The group has provided a springboard into international publishing on a large scale, and major projects overseas include a joint publishing venture with the People's Republic of China and the development of the world's first electronic book.

Kevin Weldon was the original publisher of *A day in the life of Australia*, and other successful publishing initiatives include *Australia the beautiful* series, *The designer collection*, *Above Sydney*, and *The Bradman albums*, a two volume set of cricket memorabilia from Sir Donald Bradman's personal albums. In 1982, Weldon Associates joined John Fairfax & Sons Limited and David Syme & Co to produce and market *Australians: a historical library*, the largest book publishing venture ever undertaken in Australia.

AUSTRALIANS
A HISTORICAL LIBRARY

AUSTRALIANS
A HISTORICAL LIBRARY

HISTORY PROJECT INCORPORATED STAFF

CONTRIBUTORS

Brian Adams VIII
Author
Sydney

Don Aitken VIII
Professor of Political Science
Research School of Social Sciences
Australian National University

Katrina Alford VIII
Research Fellow in Economic History
Research School of Social Sciences
Australian National University

Stephen Alomes VIII
Historian
Melbourne

Margaret Anderson II
Co-ordinator
Museum of Social History
History Trust of South Australia

Barry Andrews VIII
Senior Lecturer in English
University of New South Wales
Australian Defence Force Academy

John Andrews VIII
Teacher
Melbourne

Graeme Aplin VI, VII
Senior Lecturer in Geography
Macquarie University

Franca Arena V
Sydney

John Arnold VIII
Deputy La Trobe Librarian
State Library of Victoria

Allan Ashbolt V
Sydney

Alan Atkinson II, VIII
Senior Lecturer in History
University of New England

V. Attenbrow VI
Prehistorian
University of Sydney

Marian Aveling II
Lecturer in History
Monash University

Blair Badcock VI
Senior Lecturer in Geography
University of Adelaide

D. W. A. Baker VIII
Reader in History
Faculty of Arts
Australian National University

Susan Bambrick VIII
Senior Lecturer in Economics
Faculty of Economics and Commerce
Australian National University

Alan Barcan IX
Associate Professor of Education
University of Newcastle

Alan Barnard VIII, X
Professorial Fellow in Economic History
Research School in Social Sciences
Australian National University

Gordon Barton V
London

Diane E. Barwick VIII
Historian
Canberra

Weston Bate VII, VIII
Professor of Australian Studies
Deakin University

F. H. Bauer VII, VIII
Historical geographer
Canberra

Beryl Beaurepaire V
Melbourne

R. Bednarik VI
Editor, Rock Art Research
Elsternwick, Victoria

David Bell VI
Prehistorian
Sydney

Diane Bell I, VIII
Professor of Australian Studies
Deakin University

Tracy Bell VIII
Research Assistant
Bicentennial History Project
Research School of Social Sciences
Australian National University

J. M. Bennett VIII
Barrister-at-Law
Sydney

Paul Bentley IX
Librarian
Sydney Opera House Trust Library

Anne Bickford II
Consultant archaeologist
Sydney

Merle Bignell VII
Historian
Kojonup, WA

Terry Birtles VI, VIII
Principal Lecturer in Applied Geography
Canberra College of Advanced Education

Geoffrey Blainey I
Ernest Scott Professor of History
University of Melbourne

D. Blair IX
Lecturer in English
Macquarie University

Audrey Blake V
Westgate, NSW

Elise Blumann IV
Artist
Perth

Geoffrey Bolton VIII
Professor of History
Murdoch University

Malcolm Booker IX
Author
Canberra

D. H. Borchardt IX
Librarian and bibliographer
Melbourne

Paul Bourke III
Director
Research School of Social Sciences
Australian National University

Sandra Bowdler I
Professor of Prehistory
University of Western Australia

Ian Bowie VI
Senior Lecturer in Geography
Mitchell College of Advanced Education

J. M. Bowler I
Senior Fellow in Geomorphology
Research School of Pacific Studies
Australian National University

David Bowman VIII
Journalist
Sydney

I *To 1788* II *1838* III *1888* IV *1938* V *From 1939* VI *Historical atlas* VII *Events and places* VIII *Historical dictionary* IX *A guide to sources* X *Historical statistics* XI *The guide and index*

AUSTRALIANS
A HISTORICAL LIBRARY

E. K. Braybrooke IX
Emeritus Professor of Legal Studies
La Trobe University

R. Breckon IX
Philatelic Curator
Australia Post, Melbourne

Helen Bridge X
Research Assistant in Economic History
Faculty of Economics and Commerce
Australian National University

Alan Brissenden VIII
Reader in English
University of Adelaide

Frank Broeze II
Associate Professor of History
University of Western Australia

Geraldine Brooks VIII
Journalist
Sydney

Richard Broome VIII
Historian
Melbourne

P. L. Brown VIII
Historian
Geelong, Vic.

Beverley Burgmann IV, VIII
Researcher
Sydney

Ian H. Burnley IX
Associate Professor of Geography
University of New South Wales

N. G. Butlin VIII, X
Emeritus Professor of Economic History
Australian National University

Colin Caldwell II
Historian
Canberra

J. C. Caldwell X
Professor of Demography
Research School of Social Sciences
Australian National University

Frank Cain VIII
Senior Lecturer in History
University of New South Wales
Australian Defence Force Academy

J. M. R. Cameron II, VII
Dean
Faculty of Education
Darwin Institute of Technology

J. C. R. Camm VI, VII
Senior Lecturer in Geography
University of Newcastle

Edmund Campion VIII
Senior Lecturer in History
St Patrick's College, Manly, NSW

Richard Cashman VIII
Senior Lecturer in History
University of New South Wales

Alex C. Castles IV
Professor of Law
University of Adelaide

Axel Clark VIII
Lecturer in English
Faculty of Arts
Australian National University

John K. Clegg VI
Senior Lecturer in Anthropology
University of Sydney

Peter Cochrane IV
Lecturer in History
University of Sydney

Stewart Cockburn IV, VIII
Author and journalist
Adelaide

Mimi Colligan II
Historian
Melbourne

W. F. Connell IV
Emeritus Professor of Education
University of Sydney

C. N. Connolly VIII
Senior Lecturer in History
University of Canterbury
New Zealand

R. L. Cope IX
Librarian
New South Wales Parliamentary Library

Charles Copeman V
Sydney

Brian J. Costar VIII
Senior Lecturer in Political Studies
Chisholm Institute of Technology

Roger Covell VIII
Professor of Music
University of New South Wales

Ross Cranston VIII
Professor of Law
University of London

Victor Crittenden, VIII, IX
Librarian and bibliographer
Canberra

P. W. Crockett VIII
Historian
Melbourne

Frank Crowley VI
Emeritus Professor of History
University of New South Wales

D. Cumming IX
Senior Lecturer in Civil Engineering
University of Adelaide

Chris Cunneen VIII
Deputy General Editor
Australian Dictionary of Biography
Research School of Social Sciences
Australian National University

Ann Curthoys V
Associate Head
School of Humanities and Social Sciences
New South Wales Institute of Technology

Braham Dabscheck VIII
Senior Lecturer in Industrial Relations
University of New South Wales

Brian Dalton VII
Professor of History
James Cook University of North Queensland

M. T. Daly VI
Professor of Geography
University of Sydney

Ian Davey III
Senior Lecturer in Education
University of Adelaide

Bruce Davidson X
Senior Lecturer in Agricultural Economics
University of Sydney

Jim Davidson VIII
Historian
Melbourne

Graeme Davison III
Professor of History
Monash University

Lyndall Dawson IX
Professional Officer
University of New South Wales

David Denholm II, VII, VIII
Senior Lecturer in History
Riverina–Murray Institute
of Higher Education

P. H. de Serville VIII
Historian
Melbourne

Brian Dickey IV, VIII, X
Reader in History
Flinders University of South Australia

Don Dickson IV
formerly Lecturer in Humanities
Darwin Community College

I *To 1788* II *1838* III *1888* IV *1938* V *From 1939* VI *Historical atlas* VII *Events and places* VIII *Historical dictionary* IX *A guide to sources* X *Historical statistics* XI *The guide and index*

Marcel van Dijk X
Meteorologist
Bureau of Meteorology
Melbourne

Bob Dixon I
Professor of Linguistics
Faculty of Arts
Australian National University

Louise Douglas IV, VIII
Curator of Social History
Power House Museum, Sydney

Barrie Dyster II
Senior Lecturer in Economic History
University of New South Wales

Beverley Earnshaw II
Historian and genealogist
Sydney

Suzanne Edgar VIII
Writer
Canberra

P. G. Edwards V
Official Historian
Australian War Memorial

Richard Ely VIII
Senior Lecturer in History
University of Tasmania

Anthony M. Endres X
Senior Lecturer in Economics
University of Auckland, New Zealand

Elizabeth Evatt V
Sydney

D. R. Everingham VIII
Researcher
Sydney

R. H. Fagan VIII
Senior Lecturer in Geography
Macquarie University

Charles Fahey III
Historian
Victorian Conservation,
Forests and Lands Department

Lindsay A. Farrall VIII
Dean of Humanities
Deakin University

Frank Farrell VIII
Senior Lecturer in History
University of New South Wales

K. T. H. Farrer VIII
formerly Chief Scientist
Kraft Foods Limited
Melbourne

W. C. Ferguson I
Archaeological Consultant
ANUTECH, Canberra

Kevin Fewster VIII
Historian
Sydney

D. E. Fifer VIII
Historian
Sydney

Mark Finnane VIII
Lecturer in Humanities
Griffith University

Cecil Fisher IV
Brisbane

Ross Fitzgerald VIII
Lecturer in Humanities
Griffith University

Brian H. Fletcher VIII, IX
Associate Professor of History
University of Sydney

Marion Fletcher VIII
Author
Melbourne

Josephine Flood I
Senior Conservation Officer
Australian Heritage Commission
Canberra

Colin Forster X
Professor of Economic History
Faculty of Economics and Commerce
Australian National University

Jane Foulcher VIII
Research Historian
National Parks and Wildlife Service
Sydney

David Frankel VI
Senior Lecturer in Archaeology
La Trobe University

Andrew Frazer VIII
Research Scholar in History
Research School of Social Sciences
Australian National University

Graham Freudenberg VIII
Political writer
Sydney

Alan Frost I, VIII, IX
Reader in History
La Trobe University

Linda Frow VIII
Researcher
Sydney

E. C. Fry V
Reader in History
Faculty of Arts
Australian National University

Gavin Fry VIII
Curator
Australian War Memorial

Al Gabay VIII
Research Scholar in History
La Trobe University

Bill Gammage IV
Senior Lecturer in History
University of Adelaide

Bryan Gandevia VIII, IX
Consultant physician
Sydney

Don Garden VIII
Lecturer in History
Melbourne College of Advanced Education

Stephen Garton V
Lecturer in Humanities
Griffith University

Alex George IX
Executive Editor
Flora of Australia
Bureau of Flora and Fauna
Department of Arts,
Heritage and the Environment
Canberra

Alfie Gerrard IV
Kimberleys, WA

H. J. Gibbney VII
Historian
Canberra

Alan D. Gilbert III, IV, V
Deputy Rector and Professor of History
University of New South Wales
Australian Defence Force Academy

L. A. Gilbert VIII
formerly Principal Lecturer in History
Armidale College of Advanced Education

J. Ginswick X
Economic Historian
Sydney

Tim Godfrey VIII
Archivist
Archives of Business and Labour
Australian National University

Murray Goot VIII, X
Senior Lecturer in Politics
Macquarie University

I *To 1788* II *1838* III *1888* IV *1938* V *From 1939* VI *Historical atlas* VII *Events and places* VIII *Historical dictionary* IX *A guide to sources* X *Historical statistics* XI *The guide and index*

D. Gordon X
Professor of Social Medicine
University of Queensland

Emma Grahame VIII
Research Assistant
Australian Dictionary of Biography
Research School of Social Sciences
Australian National University

Al Grassby V
Canberra

Sheilah Gray IV
Lecturer in History
University of Newcastle

A. Graycar IX
Director
Social Welfare Research Centre
University of New South Wales

A. Green VI
Consultant
Sydney

Margaret Green VIII
Tutor in Australian Literature
Workers Education Association
Sydney

J. S. Gregory VIII
Historian
Melbourne

Patricia Grimshaw III, IV, VIII
Senior Lecturer in History
University of Melbourne

Denis Grundy X
Senior Lecturer in Education
Flinders University of South Australia

Niel Gunson VIII
Senior Fellow in Pacific History
Research School of Pacific Studies
Australian National University

Richard Haese VIII
Senior Lecturer in Art History
La Trobe University

Stephanie Hagan IX
Tutor in Politics
University of New England

A. J. Hagger IX
Honorary Research Associate in Economics
University of Tasmania

Sandra Hall VIII
Film critic and author
The *Bulletin*
Sydney

Sylvia J. Hallam I
Associate Professor of Prehistory
University of Western Australia

Valmai Hankel IX
Fine Books Librarian
State Library of South Australia

Peter Harrison VIII
Town Planner
Canberra

Sophie Harrison IV
Adelaide

Geoffrey Hawker VIII
Writer and consultant
Sydney

Laurel Heath II, VIII
Director
Curriculum Resources Centre
Canberra College of Advanced Education

R. L. Heathcote III, VI
Reader in Geography
Flinders University of South Australia

Peter Hempenstall IV, VIII
Senior Lecturer in History
University of Newcastle

G. R. Henning VIII, IX
Senior Lecturer in Economic History
University of New England

Luise Hercus VI
Reader in Asian Studies
Australian National University

H. P. Heseltine VIII
Professor of English
University of New South Wales
Australian Defence Force Academy

Neville Hicks V
Senior Lecturer in Community Medicine
University of Adelaide

B. W. Higman VIII
Professor of History
University of the West Indies
Jamaica

A. J. Hill VIII
Historian
Canberra

Eliza Hill VIII
Research Assistant
Australian Dictionary of Biography
Research School of Social Sciences
Australian National University

Kath Hinchley IV
Aurukun, Qld

J. B. Hirst III, VII
Reader in History
La Trobe University

J. E. Hobbs VI
Senior Lecturer in Geography
University of New England

J. E. Hoffman IX
Director of Public Relations
Australian Capital Territory
Schools Authority

Patricia Holt VIII
Author and public servant
Sydney

Stephen Holt VIII
Researcher
Canberra

R. W. Home IX
Professor of History
and Philosophy of Science
University of Melbourne

John Horacek IX
Senior Librarian
Borchardt Library
La Trobe University

Jack Horner IV
Writer
Canberra

M. Horsburgh IX
Associate Professor of Social Work
University of Sydney

W. J. Hudson VIII
Editor of Historical Documents
Department of Foreign Affairs
Canberra

Colin A. Hughes X
Australian Electoral Commissioner
Canberra

Lyall Hunt VIII
Senior Lecturer in Education
Western Australian College
of Advanced Education

Amirah Inglis IV, VIII
Writer
Canberra

K. S. Inglis IV, V, VI, VIII
Professor of History
Research School of Social Sciences
Australian National University

Ossie Ingram IV
Narrandera, NSW

T. H. Irving VIII
Associate Professor of Government
University of Sydney

Alick Jackomos IV
North Balwyn, Vic

I *To 1788* II *1838* III *1888* IV *1938* V *From 1939* VI *Historical atlas* VII *Events and places* VIII *Historical dictionary* IX *A guide to sources* X *Historical statistics* XI *The guide and index*

AUSTRALIANS
A HISTORICAL LIBRARY

Merle Jackomos IV
North Balwyn, Vic

R. Jackson X
Senior Lecturer in Economic History
Faculty of Economics and Commerce
Australian National University

Dean Jaensch X
Reader in Politics
Flinders University of South Australia

D. N. Jeans IV, VI
Associate Professor of Geography
University of Sydney

Keith Johnson IX
President
Society of Australian Genealogists
Sydney

Lesley Johnson IV
Lecturer in Education
University of Melbourne

W. Ross Johnston VII
Associate Professor of History
University of Queensland

L. J. Jones IX
Senior Lecturer in Mechanical
and Industrial Engineering
University of Melbourne

Ann-Mari Jordens VIII
Senior Research Officer
Official History Unit
Australian War Memorial

Eugene Kamenka VIII
Professor of the History of Ideas
Research School of Social Sciences
Australian National University

Doreen Kartinyeri IV
Historian
Adelaide

Frank Kellaway IV
Novelist
Tebbut, Vic

Roger Kellaway VII
Senior Tutor in Geography
University of Tasmania

Paul Kelly VIII
Associate Editor
Sydney Morning Herald

Brian Kennedy VIII
Senior Lecturer in History
Monash University

K. H. Kennedy VIII
Senior Lecturer in History
James Cook University of North Queensland

Charles Kerr VI
Professor of Health and Tropical Medicine
University of Sydney

Joan Kerr II, VIII, IX
Associate Professor of Fine Arts
University of Sydney

A. P. Kershaw X
Senior Lecturer in Geography
Monash University

R. G. Kimber I, VII
Author
Alice Springs

Hazel King VIII
Historian
Sydney

Jonathan King VIII
Historian, author and university lecturer
Sydney

John Knott VIII
Lecturer in History
Faculty of Arts
Australian National University

James Kohen I
Research Scholar in Prehistory
Macquarie University

Rick Kuhn VIII
Economist
Bureau of Industry Economics
Department of Industry and Commerce
Canberra

John Lack IV
Lecturer in History
University of Melbourne

Marilyn Lake VIII
Lecturer in History
University of Melbourne

R. J. Lampert I, VI
Curator of Anthropology
The Australian Museum

H. Lancaster X
Emeritus Professor of Mathematical Statistics
University of Sydney

Diane Langmore VIII
Research Editor
Australian Dictionary of Biography
Research School of Social Sciences
Australian National University

Marcia Langton IV
Co-ordinator of Land Tenure
Central Lands Council
Alice Springs, NT

Alan Lawson IX
Lecturer in English
University of Queensland

Sylvia Lawson V
Lecturer in Humanities
Griffith University

Lenore Layman IV, VIII
Lecturer in History
Murdoch University

Jane Lee IX
Librarian
Department of Foreign Affairs
Canberra

Miles Lewis VIII
Senior Lecturer in Architecture and Building
University of Melbourne

G. J. R. Ling VIII
Professorial Fellow in Human Geography
Research School of Pacific Studies
Australian National University

Rob Linn II, VIII
Historian
Adelaide

Carol Liston VIII
Historian
Sydney

Shirley Lithgow VIII
Historian
Canberra

M. Lorimer IX
Canberra

Alan Lougheed X
Senior Lecturer in Economics
University of Queensland

Harry Lourandos I
Lecturer in Prehistory
University of Queensland

Peter Love VIII, IX
Historian
Yan Yean, Vic

Isabel McBryde I
Professor of Prehistory
Faculty of Arts
Australian National University

J. W. McCarty III
Professor of Economic History
Monash University

Murray McCaskill VI
Professor of Geography
Flinders University of South Australia

I *To 1788* II *1838* III *1888* IV *1938* V *From 1939* VI *Historical atlas* VII *Events and places* VIII *Historical dictionary* IX *A guide to sources* X *Historical statistics* XI *The guide and index.*

J. MacCulloch VIII
Researcher
Sydney

Alison McCusker IX
Assistant Secretary
Conservation Branch
Department of Arts, Heritage and the Environment
Canberra

G. MacDonald VI
Archaeologist
Sydney

Lorna McDonald VII
Historian
Rockhampton, Qld

Peter McDonald VIII, X
Deputy Director of Planning and Research
Institute of Family Studies
Melbourne

Ellen McEwen III
Historian
Sydney

Ann McGrath IV, IX
Lecturer in History
University of New South Wales

Lawrence D. McIntosh IX
Librarian
Joint Theological Library
Ormond College
University of Melbourne

Stuart Macintyre VIII, IX
Senior Lecturer in History
University of Melbourne

Michael McKernan IX, X
Assistant Director
Research and Publications
Australian War Memorial

Susan McKernan VIII
Lecturer in English
University of New South Wales
Australian Defence Force Academy

Robin McLachlan VII
Lecturer in Communication and Liberal Studies
Mitchell College of Advanced Education

Ian F. McLaren IX
Honorary Bibliographer
Baillieu Library
University of Melbourne

Ian W. McLean VIII, X
Senior Lecturer in Economics
University of Adelaide

Ailsa McLeary III
Historian
Melbourne

W. G. McMinn VIII
Associate Professor of History
University of Newcastle

John McQuilton VI, VII, VIII, IX
Senior Project Officer
Department of Geography
University of New South Wales
Australian Defence Force Academy

Rodney Maddock V
Professor of Economics
Universidad de Antioguia
Colombia

Ian Maddocks IV
Medical practitioner
Adelaide

Graham Maddox IX
Senior Lecturer in Politics
University of New England

Reg Mahoney IV
Wollongong

Andrew Markus IV, VIII, IX
Lecturer in History
Monash University

Julie G. Marshall IX
Reference Librarian
Borchardt Library
La Trobe University

A. W. Martin III, V, VIII, IX
Senior Fellow in History
Research School of Social Sciences
Australian National University

Ged Martin VIII
Director
Centre of Canadian Studies
University of Edinburgh

Isolde Martyn VII
Historian
Sydney

Dawn May IV
Historian
Townsville, Qld

Henry Mayer IX
Emeritus Professor of Political Theory
University of Sydney

Diane Menghetti IV
Lecturer in History
James Cook University of North Queensland

John Merritt VIII
Senior Lecturer in History
Faculty of Arts
Australian National University

T. B. Millar VIII, IX
Professor of Australian Studies
Australian Studies Centre
London

Carol M. Mills IX
Institute Librarian
Riverina-Murray Institute of Higher Education

Hans Mincham VII
Author
Adelaide

Bruce Mitchell VIII
Senior Lecturer in History
University of New England

Winifred Mitchell IV
Historian
Wollongong

Frances Morphy I
Research Assistant in Linguistics
Faculty of Arts
Australian National University

Howard Morphy I, V
Senior Lecturer in Anthropology
Faculty of Arts
Australian National University

John Morton VIII
Postdoctoral Fellow in Anthropology
Research School of Pacific Studies
Australian National University

Marcie Muir IX
Author
Adelaide

S. K. Mukherjee X
Principal Criminologist
Australian Institute of Criminology
Canberra

D. J. Mulvaney I, VIII
Emeritus Professor of Prehistory
Australian National University

Stephen Murray-Smith V
Mt Eliza, Vic

Elizabeth Nathan IX
Head
Archives Section
Department of Foreign Affairs
Canberra

Hank Nelson IV, V
Senior Fellow in Pacific History
Research School of Pacific Studies
Australian National University

Max Neutze VI, VIII
Professor of Urban Research
Research School of Social Sciences
Australian National University

Richard Neville II
Art historian
Sydney

Richard A. Nile VIII
Historian and tutor
University of New South Wales

Frances O'Donoghue II
Lecturer in History
Catholic Institute of Faith
Brisbane

Patrick O'Farrell VIII
Professor of History
University of New South Wales

John O'Hara VIII
Senior Lecturer in History
Tasmanian State Institute of Technology

Bernard O'Neil II, IV, VIII
Historian and editor
Adelaide

Julian Oppenheimer II, VII, VIII
Historian and grazier
Walcha, NSW

Mabel Pamulkan IV
Aurukun, Qld

G. Parkinson VI
Chief Geographer
Division of National Mapping
Canberra

G. Peguero IX
Chief Librarian
Phillip Institute of Technology, Vic

P. A. Pemberton VIII
Deputy Archives Officer
Archives of Business and Labour
Australian National University

T. M. Perry VI, X
Professor of Geography
University of Melbourne

Mary Pescott VIII
Teacher
Brisbane

N. Peterson VI, IX
Senior Lecturer in Prehistory
Faculty of Arts
Australian National University

David Philips III
Senior Lecturer in History
University of Melbourne

W. W. Phillips X
Senior Lecturer in History
La Trobe University

Graeme Phipps IX
Curator of Birds
Zoological Parks Board of New South Wales

Stuart Piggin IX
Senior Lecturer in History
University of Wollongong

J. J. Pincus VIII
Professor of Economic History
Flinders University of South Australia

John Playford VIII
Senior Lecturer in Politics
University of Adelaide

N. J. B. Plomley VIII
Biologist and historian
Queen Victoria Museum
Launceston, Tas

Carolyn Polizzotto IV
Historian
Perth

David Pope X
Associate Professor of Economic History
University of New South Wales

E. Daniel Potts VIII
Associate Professor of History
Monash University

Alan Powell VII, VIII
Professor of History and Dean of Arts
University College of the Northern Territory

J. M. Powell VII, VIII, IX
Reader in Geography
Monash University

Charles Price X
formerly Professorial Fellow in Demography
Research School of Social Sciences
Australian National University

Susan Priestley VII
Historian
Melbourne

J. R. V. Prescott VI
Reader in Geography
University of Melbourne

Patricia Pyne X
Research Assistant in Demography
Research School of Social Sciences
Australian National University

Geoffrey Raby X
formerly Lecturer in Economics
La Trobe University

Heather Radi VIII
Historian
Sydney

Don Rawson VIII
Senior Fellow in Political Science
Research School of Social Sciences
Australian National University

Pamela Ray IX
Manuscripts Librarian
National Library of Australia

A. J. Rayner II
Historian
Hobart

Harry Rayner VIII
Journalist
Canberra

Gail Reekie IV, VIII
Researcher
Sydney

Andrew Reeves VIII
Deputy Director
Museum of Victoria

Kerreen Reiger IV
Lecturer in Sociology
Phillip Institute of Technology, Vic

Barry Reynolds I
Professor of Material Culture
James Cook University of North Queensland

Henry Reynolds III
Associate Professor of History
James Cook University of North Queensland

Len Richardson VIII
Senior Lecturer in History
University of Canterbury
New Zealand

John Rickard IV, VIII
Associate Professor of History
Monash University

P. Rimmer IX
Senior Fellow in Human Geography
Research School of Pacific Studies
Australian National University

C. S. Ripper VIII
Field Officer
Water Resources Commission
Griffith, NSW

John Ritchie VIII
Senior Lecturer in History
Faculty of Arts
Australian National University

John Robertson VIII
Associate Professor of History
University of New South Wales
Australian Defence Force Academy

L. L. Robson VIII
Reader in History
University of Melbourne

Michael Roe VIII, IX
Professor of History
University of Tasmania

A. Ross VI
Prehistorian
Sydney

D. T. Rowland VIII
Lecturer in Population Studies
Faculty of Arts
Australian National University

Tim Rowse V
Writer and researcher
Sydney

H. M. Russell IX
Director
Scientific and Information Services
Department of Agriculture
Victoria

Lado Ruzicka X
formerly Professorial Fellow in Demography
Research School of Social Sciences
Australian National University

Lyndall Ryan I, II
Reader in Women's Studies
Flinders University of South Australia

Joan Rydon IX
Professor of Politics
La Trobe University

Hugh Saddler X
Consultant and Director
Energy Policy and Analysis Pty Ltd
Canberra

Leonie Sandercock IV
Professor of Urban Studies
Macquarie University

David Saunders IX
Professor of Architecture
University of Adelaide

G. Sawer VIII
Emeritus Professor of Law
Australian National University

D. M. Schreuder III
Challis Professor of History
University of Sydney

Clement Semmler VIII
Writer
Bowral, NSW

Geoffrey Serle VIII
General Editor
Australian Dictionary of Biography
Research School of Social Sciences
Australian National University

Michael Sexton VIII
Lawyer and author
Sydney

A. G. L. Shaw VIII, IX
Emeritus Professor of History
Monash University

Bruce Shaw IV
Writer
Bridgewater, SA

G. P. Shaw VIII
Reader in History
University of Queensland

Peter Shergold X
Senior Lecturer in Economic History
University of New South Wales

Tom Sheridan V
Senior Lecturer in Economics
University of Adelaide

Geoffrey Sherington IV
Senior Lecturer in Education
University of Sydney

Adam Shoemaker, VIII
Assistant Director, Survey
Australian Archives

Adrienne Short VIII
Research Assistant
Bicentennial History Project
Research School of Social Sciences
Australian National University

W. A. Sinclair IX
Dean of the Faculty of Economics and Commerce
Monash University

F. B. Smith IV, VIII
Professorial Fellow in History
Research School of Social Sciences
Australian National University

M. A. Smith I
Field Archaeologist
Museums and Art Galleries of the Northern Territory
Alice Springs

Philippa Mein Smith VIII
Research Scholar in History
Research School of Social Sciences
Australian National University

Terry Smith IX
Senior Lecturer in Fine Arts
University of Sydney

Graeme Snooks X
Reader in Economic History
Flinders University of South Australia

R. J. Solomon VI, VII
Geographer and consultant
Sydney

Gavin Souter IV, VIII
Historian and journalist
Sydney

O. H. K. Spate VIII
Emeritus Professor of Pacific History
Australian National University

Andrew Spaull IV, VIII
Reader in Education
Monash University

Peter Spearritt IV, V, VI, VIII, IX
Associate Professor of Politics
Macquarie University

G. F. R. Spenceley V, VIII
Senior Lecturer in Economic History
Monash University

Tom Stannage IV
Associate Professor of History
University of Western Australia

Maisy Stapleton IV
Project Co-ordinator
Campbell Associates
Sydney

Graeme Starr VIII
State Director
Liberal Party of Australia
NSW Division

Pamela Statham X
Senior Lecturer in Economic History
University of Western Australia

Marion K. Stell VIII, IX
Research Assistant
Department of History
Research School of Social Sciences
Australian National University

Margaret Steven VIII
Historian
Canberra

Frank Stilwell V
Associate Professor of Economics
University of Sydney

Brian Stoddart IV
Senior Lecturer in Sports Studies
Canberra College of Advanced Education

Lurline Stuart VIII
Writer and bibliographer
Melbourne

Martin Sullivan II
Senior Lecturer in Education
Monash University

Kyra Suthern X
Research Officer in Economic History
Research School of Social Sciences
Australian National University

Peter Sutton VI
Consulting Anthropologist
Adelaide

Malcolm Thomis VII, VIII
Professor of History
University of Queensland

Ruth Thompson IV, VIII
Writer
Sydney

R. Tonkinson I
Professor of Anthropology
University of Western Australia

P. R. Trier IX
Principal Librarian
Baillieu Library
University of Melbourne

T. G. Vallance IX
Associate Professor of Geology and Geophysics
University of Sydney

Wray Vamplew X
Reader in Economic History
Flinders University of South Australia

P. J. N. Varghese VIII
Foreign Affairs Officer
Department of Foreign Affairs
Canberra

Pat Vinnicombe VI
Research Officer
Department of Aboriginal Sites
Western Australian Museum

D. A. Wadley IX
Senior Lecturer in Geography
University of Queensland

David Walker III, IV
Senior Lecturer in History
University of New South Wales

J. D. Walker VIII
Historical Officer
Department of Aviation
Canberra

Kath Walker V
Sydney

R. B. Walker VIII
Associate Professor of History
Macquarie University

G. P. Walsh VIII
Senior Lecturer in History
University of New South Wales
Australian Defence Force Academy

Michael Walsh VI
Senior Lecturer in Linguistics
University of Sydney

J. L. Ward IX
formerly Chief Librarian
Royal Melbourne Institute of Technology

John Manning Ward VIII
Vice-Chancellor and Principal
University of Sydney

John Warhurst V
Professor of Politics
University of New England

Duncan Waterson VII
Professor of History
Macquarie University

Kimberley Webber VIII
Senior Tutor in Museum Studies
University of Sydney

Elizabeth Webby II, VIII
Associate Professor of English
University of Sydney

Patrick Weller VIII
Professor of Public Policy
School of Social and Industrial Administration
Griffith University

R. L. Wettenhall IX
Head of Administrative Studies
Canberra College of Advanced Education

J. Peter White I
Reader in Prehistory
University of Sydney

Kate White VIII
Author
Melbourne

Richard White IV, VIII
Historian
Sydney

Stephen A. Wild I
Ethnomusicologist
Australian Institute of Aboriginal Studies
Canberra

William H. Wilde VIII
Associate Professor of English
University of New South Wales
Australian Defence Force Academy

G. L. Wilkenfeld VIII
Policy Analyst
Energy Authority of NSW

Beth Williams IV
Sydney

Elizabeth Williams VI
Research Scholar
Department of Prehistory and Anthropology
Australian National University

Janis Wilton IV
Lecturer
Centre for Social Science Education
Armidale College of Advanced Education

Elizabeth Windshuttle II
Research Scholar in History
University of New South Wales

Judy Wing VIII
Researcher
Sydney

Glen Withers X
Professor of Economics
La Trobe University

D. I. Wright VIII
Senior Lecturer in History
University of Newcastle

Judith Wright VIII
Author
Mongarlowe via Braidwood, NSW

D. Wyndham IX
Head
Research and Information
Australian Film, Television and Radio School
Sydney

A. T. Yarwood VIII
Historian
Paradise Point, Qld

G. Young VI
Senior Lecturer in Architecture and Building
South Australian Institute of Technology

F. F. F. Yuan X
Lecturer in General Studies
South Australian Institute of Technology

I *To 1788* II *1838* III *1888* IV *1938* V *From 1939* VI *Historical atlas* VII *Events and places* VIII *Historical dictionary* IX *A guide to sources* X *Historical statistics* XI *The guide and index*

AUSTRALIANS
A HISTORICAL LIBRARY

GENERAL EDITORS

ALAN D. GILBERT   K. S. INGLIS

ASSISTANT GENERAL EDITOR

S. G. FOSTER

AUSTRALIANS TO 1788

AUSTRALIANS 1838

AUSTRALIANS 1888

AUSTRALIANS 1938

AUSTRALIANS FROM 1939

GENERAL EDITORS

FRANK CROWLEY   PETER SPEARRITT

ASSISTANT GENERAL EDITOR

JOHN MCQUILTON

AUSTRALIANS
A HISTORICAL ATLAS

AUSTRALIANS
A HISTORICAL DICTIONARY

AUSTRALIANS
EVENTS AND PLACES

AUSTRALIANS
HISTORICAL STATISTICS

AUSTRALIANS
A GUIDE TO SOURCES

EXECUTIVE EDITOR

S. G. FOSTER

CONTENTS

INTRODUCTION

*A*USTRALIANS: *THE GUIDE AND INDEX* provides a single access point to the eleven volumes of *Australians: a historical library*. This volume also contains a number of reference lists: people who have held high office in federal and state governments; winners of awards and honours related to the arts and to community life; and achievements in major Australian and international sporting events.

Each book in *Australians: a historical library* stands alone and can be read as a separate work. Each provides a unique vision of the past. The editors and contributors have approached the task of illuminating Australia's past in a variety of ways. In *Australians to 1788*, for example, the long period of Aboriginal occupation of the continent has been surveyed using the skills and knowledge of prehistorians, archaeologists, anthropologists, linguists and other experts; written records have been combined with Aboriginal oral history and material evidence of Aboriginal culture. The three 'slice' volumes—*1838*, *1888* and *1938*—focus on particular years, with special concern for the lives of ordinary people. *Australians from 1939* surveys the past fifty years in a broad sweep, using a wide range of resources, from traditional historical records to the recollections, both oral and written, of many kinds of people.

The reference volumes are similarly diverse in purpose and structure. The *Historical atlas* uses a range of cartographic techniques to provide a visual record of the evolution of the Australian landscape. *Events and places* provides a succinct chronology of Australian history and a historical gazetteer. The *Historical dictionary* organises the past into more than a thousand subject and biographical entries. *A guide to sources* provides an overview of how Australia's past has been revealed in thousands of publications. *Historical statistics* presents a detailed tabular and graphic record of Australian life.

The books have been planned and written as a series, so that each volume complements its companions. Because the editors and contributors have largely taken a thematic approach, the series can be dipped into and browsed through. You can, for example, read about the lives of working people—townsfolk and sailors, farmers and graziers—in chapter 4 of *1838* and compare their experiences with people at work in section II of *1888*—on farms and stations, in mines and the capital cities—and in section IV of *1938*, which considers the lives of country people, labourers, steelworkers and others as diverse as detectives, canecutters and journalists.

Similarly, the lives of the unemployed in 1888 are typified by Thomas Dobeson, whose experience is chronicled on pages 204–7 of *Australians 1888*. Vital to this account are the photographs of the Dobeson family and the Dobeson home—no mere decorations but an intrinsic element in the telling of the story. The unemployed of 1938 are visited in chapter 22 of that volume. Statistics about unemployment are presented on pages 150–54 of chapter 9 of *Historical statistics*; there is a general chronological survey of unemployment in the entry of that name in the *Historical dictionary*; and unemployment during the Great Depression is mapped in detail in chapter 12 of the *Atlas*.

Each book has its own index which provides access to the material within it. The index for the *Historical dictionary*, for example, indicates the main entry for cricket (pages 97–98), the entries for the Ashes (page 19), bodyline (page 49), Sir Donald Bradman (pages 54–55), the Chappell brothers (page 72), the Sheffield Shield (page 363) and Frederick Spofforth (page 378), as well as providing cross-references to World Series Cricket and Aboriginal cricketers.

The historical gazetteer in *Events and places* is arranged by regions, which are listed on pages ix–x and shown on the map on page 213. To get to know a region, begin from either of these two access points and from there move to the general survey of the region and thence to a study of the individual places, which are arranged alphabetically within each region. The list of resources in the 'Suggested reading' section provides further extension. For quick reference, and if you are unsure which region a specific place is in, use the place index on pages 474–76. For a subject approach, consult the *Guide and index*.

The general index in this volume brings together the individual volume indexes to provide a selective but detailed access point for the entire series. As noted in the examples above, broad themes can be pursued through either the contents pages or the indexes of the various volumes. Thematic information can also be traced through the general index in this *Guide*, which complements and extends the volume indexes. It invites the reader to use *Australians: a historical library* as a wide-ranging historical work, addressing the larger issues of Australian history as well as describing in fine detail the daily lives of past generations.

Housing, for example, is a theme common to all the volumes, each of which treats this subject in its own way and from a particular perspective. By using the general index in this volume, the reader gains access to the many discussions of housing throughout the series. In *Australians to 1788*, for example, 'Waiting for the Djirrapuyngu', reconstructs a time in the life of an Arnhem Land Aborigine, with a description of his home and later photographs of similar homes in the region. 'Work in the towns' on pages 129–36 of *1838*, discusses the problems associated with building houses in the embryonic colonial capitals, illustrated with sketches and paintings and accompanied by a graphic description from a contemporary observer of how to build a house.

The general index refers the reader to a discussion in *1888* of 'The suburban frontier' (pages 220–27), the epitome of late Victorian urban development. The index also directs the reader to external and internal views of contemporary housing (on pages 213, 313–16), and photographs of a country cottage (page 233) and grand house (page 138). The *1938* volume devotes an entire chapter—'Emoh ruo'—to housing, again illustrated with contemporary sketches, plans, advertisements and photographs. This is followed, on page 139, by a shorter piece, 'Building on trust', which looks specifically at the work of the South Australian Housing Trust. In *Australians from 1939* housing is again discussed—in detail between pages 86 and 90 and as part of wider themes sporadically throughout. These references can all be traced through the general index in this volume.

The *Historical atlas* maps, on pages 86–7, the changing use of building materials throughout the continent in 1901, 1933 and 1976, and devotes the following page to sketches of various kinds of rural dwellings. The *Historical dictionary* carries a thousand-word illustrated article under the entry 'Housing' and an article of similar length under 'Architecture', both of which can be traced through this general index. Historical statistics devotes a chapter to housing. This 14-page analysis begins with a general survey of changes in Australian housing and continues with tabular and graphic details of such elements as materials, numbers, sizes, costs and rentals of homes since 1851. Chapter 53 of *A guide to sources* consists of a literature survey on books about Australian architecture and an annotated listing of some fifty books about architecture and building styles, both historical and contemporary.

The importance of distance in Australia's history, and the development of various means of transport and communication to conquer that distance, are significant and challenging themes, worthy of consideration by student and non-specialist alike. The general index in this volume brings together the various treatments of transport and communication in the series. It directs the reader, for example, to Isabel McBryde's study of Aboriginal trade and exchange networks in chapter 13 of *Australians to 1788*, as well as to a discussion of Aboriginal links with the north in 'The end of the beginning' (pages 94–101) and an extensive survey of European exploration and colonisation from 1400 to 1788 in chapter 19, 'Towards Australia'.

Transport in 1838 is discussed in a section (pages 184–91) of the chapter entitled 'Markets', where it is considered as an integral part of the commercial workings of the colonies. The editors of *1888* believed the concept of 'distance' to be so significant to the nature of the Australian colonies that they devoted an entire chapter—simply named 'Distance'—to a survey of changing ways of crossing the land and moving around it by sea. A later chapter, 'People moving', shows how Australians in 1888 utilised various forms of transport to move about the country in search of work or wealth.

By 1938 the world had changed again, and the horizons of many Australians had broadened to take in a holiday 'overseas'. This phenomenon is examined in a chapter of that name (pages 435–45) in *1938*. The gatefold in that volume, too,—the *Spirit of Progress*—illustrates transport in 1938. *Australians from 1939* devotes two significant sections—'Cars for the people' (pages 119–29) and 'Press, radio and television' (pages 215–37)—to changes in transport and communication since World War II.

The general index in this volume also directs the reader to information about transport and communication in the reference volumes. There are index entries, for example, for the maps and graphs about railway development on pages 128–29 of the *Historical atlas*, and for the page of information about roads on page 130. Chapter 10 of *Historical statistics* (pages 166–82), which provides a wealth of statistical detail on transport and communication, is similarly indexed. The *Historical dictionary* includes an extensive entry on transport, and subsidiary entries on associated subjects, all of which are indexed in the general index. Similarly, the general index will direct the reader to two relevant chapters in *A guide to sources*: 'Transport' (chapter 33) and 'Post and telecommunications' (chapter 34). Each of these provides a literature survey and annotated listing of books for further reading.

The general index is not merely an amalgam of the indexes of the several volumes of *Australians: a historical library*. In fact, its entries differ significantly from those indexed in the individual volumes. Under 'Lang, John Dunmore' in the general index the reader will find reference to an entry in the *Dictionary* for a biography of Lang (page 228), a series of pages references to *1838* and *Events and places* for more information about his work in the colony, as well as a reference to his portrait in the *Sources* volume (page 15). Similarly, biographies of artists are illustrated by reference to examples of their work throughout the other volumes. In this index you will find, for example, a reference to the biographical entry about S.T. Gill on page 171 of the *Dictionary*, itself supported by a reproduction of one of his paintings. Other entries refer the reader to several of his paintings reproduced in *1838*.

Unlike the volume indexes, the general index excludes the names of people who are significant less on their own account than as part of a larger theme or argument. For example, Mary Noonan, apprenticed to Mrs Douglass, a Sydney dressmaker, in 1838, would not be entered under 'Noonan, Mary'. The reader could, however, expect to find references to her under entries such as 'apprenticeship' or 'immigration', 'indenture system' or under 'employment'. The criterion for inclusion in this general index has thus been the significance of a person, event or theme in the broad context of Australian history.

The same applies to subjects. Under 'Perth' for example, you will find a reference to page 93 of *Australians: a historical atlas*, where the city's development is traced, and pages 452–53 of *Events and places*, where a major entry on Perth is located. A passing reference to Perth as a source of holiday travel in the introduction to the 'Transport and communication' chapter of *Historical statistics* would not be indexed here; nor would a brief reference to the city in a general comment on political developments of the 1970s in *From 1939*.

The general index accentuates the pluralistic nature, not only of this series, but of Australian historical study as a whole. It refers the reader to all significant discussions of a given subject within, and beyond the series, however strongly or subtly the individual authors disagree and however different their choice of emphasis. The extension of this discussion to material beyond the series is confined largely to *A guide to sources*. This willingness to accept many possible standpoints, and this desire to present as many of those standpoints as can be encompassed in ten volumes, constitute the fresh vision *Australians* seeks to present to the nation to mark the Bicentennial year.

ACKNOWLEDGMENTS

Australians: A Historical Library includes contributions from members of every university in Australia and many other tertiary institutions. The project's Management Committees wish particularly to acknowledge the role of the Research School of Social Sciences in the Australian National University, and its successive Directors, professors Youngson, Neutze and Bourke. Also, thanks are due to the Business Manager, Peter Grimshaw, and his staff for their valuable assistance. The University of New South Wales was home to the project's Reference Section from 1979 to 1985, and continued to provide support through the University College in the Australian Defence Force Academy. The Australian Research Grants Scheme assisted research on several volumes.

The willing help of libraries, archives and galleries throughout Australia has been essential to the project's success. The Management Committees thank the many institutions who waived copyright fees or provided expert advice on illustrative material, especially the National Library of Australia, the Mitchell Library in the State Library of New South Wales, John Fairfax and Sons photo library and their Feature Services Division, Fairfax Magazines, especially Douglas Sellick, whose helpfulness and expertise led to many unpublished photographs and other source materials, and Weldon Trannies, which provided many of the contemporary photographs.

The committees also thank the following owners of copyright in pictorial material: the Julian Ashton Art School, for works by Julian Ashton; the Commercial Representatives' and Agents' Association of Australia Ltd, for *Australia Today*; and Neville Wallace, for posters used in *Australians from 1939*, Robert Holmes à Court for the Robert Holmes à Court Collection, Mrs Percy Trompf for the estate of Percy Trompf.

The committees and editors thank the following people for their help on the project and with specific volumes: Ria de Groot, Kristina Evans, Katrina Gilluley and Shirley Lithgow; Michael Pitt, Deborah Johnston, Michael O'Rourke and Gordon Stoermer; Robert Edwards and Ivan Heskovec (for help with *Australians*

Ian Berryman and A. C. Staples (*1838*); Ruth Thompson (*1938*); Bob Ceveri (*From 1939*); Marion Le Cheminant (*From 1939*); J. S. Duncan (*A Historical Atlas*); Kimberley Webber (*A Historical Dictionary*); and Michael Harrington (*A Guide to Sources*). A special thanks to Andrew Markus for editing Section II in *Australians 1938*.

Many hands have been involved in the production of these volumes. The books are wholly produced in Australia. Mark David of Griffin Press, typesetters Abbtype, who set the tables for *Historical Statistics* and Walter Deblaere all deserve special mention. The colour separations required enormous organisation and thanks are due to Peter O'Hanlon, Peter Maguire and Peter Dadour of Colour Scanners. The books have been printed in South Australia by Griffin Press and without the expertise of Gus Nancarrow and the perseverance of Bob Crane, it would not have been possible to print the books in Australia. Pat O'Malley, Ray Mules and Max Richards, also of Griffin Press, provided valuable help and advice.

Finally, a special thanks must go to Marion K. Stell, for her untiring, immediate, and efficient response to constant editorial demands from both the publisher's and authors' editors.

The Making of
Australians: A Historical Library
A Personal Retrospect

Oliver MacDonagh

W HEN I BECAME head of the Department of History at the Research School of Social Sciences at the Australian National University in 1976, my first task seemed to be to find some major undertaking which our department—as the only 'national' department in Australia, and the only department primarily devoted to research—could promote and nurture. Our existing offspring, or at least stepchild, the *Australian dictionary of biography*, already well into its second decade of distinguished work, offered an encouraging precedent.

The 1970s as well as the 1980s were an epoch of centenaries in Australia, and I had come fresh from serving on the executive committee of the multivolumed project for *A new history of Ireland*. Given this combination of circumstances, it is not surprising that my first idea for the department should have been an Australian equivalent to the *New history*, to be published in 1988 to mark the Bicentenary of the European settlement of that continent.

Even my small experience of the *A new history of Ireland* suggested to me, first, that even a decade's preparation would not be too long for any similar venture; secondly, that some mechanisms for eliminating laggard authors and replacing them in time would have to be devised and enforced; thirdly, that a considerable annual budget ($100 000 per annum for ten years was the figure plucked from the air) was indispensable; and fourthly, that auxiliary or reference volumes would form a more important element in an Australian than in an Irish scheme, because of the relative paucity, then, of source work in Australian history, and the relatively short period of time which would be covered by the history proper.

Specifically, the initial sketch plan was for eight volumes in all, four covering Australian history between 1788 and, say, 1970, with four reference books, a chronology, a historical atlas, a bibliography and a collection of historical statistics. In form, this first back-of-an-envelope scribble came remarkably close to the final outcome. But in substance the project was to change profoundly in several ways.

At this point I discovered that some sort of commemorative history for the Bicentenary had been mooted earlier at the ANU by John Molony, head of the Department of History in the Arts Faculty, but without evoking much response. Nonetheless, we tried again and on 8 October 1976 half-a-dozen of the senior historians at the university met to consider the new proposal. The crucial happening of this meeting—for the absence of a decision to smother the infant at birth can scarcely be termed a happening—was Ken Inglis's proposal that, instead of four narrative volumes, the histories should be four 'slices' of particular years: 1788, 1838, 1888 and 1938. The project was not to be an attempted summation of current scholarship, but a revolutionary type of historiography. I have a lifetime of academic meetings to remember, but this was the only occasion that I can recall when a daring, original idea was accepted with excited acclamation within thirty seconds of its being set out.

The crucial problem, as it seemed at this initial meeting, was to prevent the project being, or even being seen as, an exclusively ANU undertaking. We wished to be truly national. We feared that people in the state universities might resent our taking so bold and universal an initiative. But in the end we bit the bullet, and decided that while the editorial work should be devolved and distributed as widely as possible among the states, and while we should try to entice contributions from every part of Australia, the Research School would have to remain the controller of, and headquarters for, the project—'with', as the minutes of that first meeting ran, 'all the odium but also all the advantages which this would involve'. Perhaps I might add here the final item of those minutes (which I wrote myself): 'It was accepted that the author of these notes was, in effect, the pin in the grenade, to be discarded shortly before explosion'. For good or ill, I failed to carry this point later, and became instead the chairman of the Management Committee.

There followed some eighteen months of wooing the historical profession, stumping the country for support, attempting to appease opponents and counter critics, and lobbying the federal government for grants. To deal with the last first, despite years of soliciting and the painful preparation of an untold number of financial estimates and submissions, we never secured a penny from any state or federal department. The basic difficulty was not ill-will or scepticism about the value of the project but simply that government ministers and bureaucrats think, at most, two or three years ahead, and our time-span fitted no official budget. Had we begun in 1984 or 1985 there is no doubt whatever—in my mind at least—that we would have received the government million-dollar grant which we had counted on originally. But if we had begun in 1984 or 1985 there would have been no project ready in time for the Bicentenary.

It also seemed at first that we had been over-sanguine in expecting even substantial support and commitment from the Australian historical profession. True, our initial step—inviting, in February 1977, the head of every history department in the country to Canberra in order to consider and (they and God willing!) endorse the project—was smoothly taken. The atmosphere was genial. The scheme itself was warmly approved, as well as usefully elaborated, and the body turned itself into an interim Management Committee.

But the appearance of enthusiastic unanimity was deceptive. One or two of the departmental heads sang very different tunes when they returned to their constituents—not unlike nineteenth-century Irish MPs when they had left behind the blandishments of London and Westminster and faced the public in Clare or Mayo. In one or two other cases, departments soon made it clear that *they* by no means agreed with their respective heads. There were, besides, protests from particular interests, such as women's history, against their having no voice, and perhaps no sympathisers, in the interim Management Committee. Marxist, Foucaultist and other radical historians considered the project vitiated by the likely predominance of liberal pragmatists—'mindless empiricists' was the phrase then in vogue. Again, how *could* the project avoid being celebratory, and what was there to celebrate in the establishment of a penal settlement and the destruction of an indigenous culture?

There was moreover a powerful school of 'senior' and conservative criticism. The very senior historians had already been excluded—not greatly to their satisfaction—by one of the first decisions which we took—namely to recruit no-one as a contributor who had already passed the age of fifty-five. But even some less venerable seniors decried the project as monopolistic—one deploring it as 'the sole scholarly focus of an enormous investment, both of professional energy and government money'. It was also decried as eccentric or idiosyncratic in concentrating on arbitrarily selected segments of time at the expense of the historian's proper procedures, which were the use of the narrative method and a linear time perspective. Finally, even some who wished us well thought that the dream of harnessing teams of historians to work to the same end by absolutely immutable dates was madness.

Although painful at the time, this gallimaufry of opposition, misunderstanding, wrong-headedness, right-headedness, penetrating and obtuse criticism proved of the utmost value in the end. Late in 1977 Ken Inglis returned to Canberra from a tour of most universities quite daunted, and even dismayed, by the various receptions which our scheme had met. But in fact several of the most doubting Thomases turned out to be crucial supporters of the project later on. We were fortunate to have been baptised by fire. We were fortunate to have been taught salutary lessons in time. More precisely, the scepticism, questioning and hostility focused our attention on points already mooted but in danger of being lost to sight in the multitude of early considerations.

First, the testing of the waters brought home to us the necessity—in Australia, at any rate—of a much more democratic structure and procedure than was customary in large-scale historical undertakings. The volumes—and especially the slice volumes, which were now termed Section A—would have to grow from below rather than be imposed from above. This meant that, within the general, overarching principles of the operation, there might be considerable variety of emphasis and very different forms of teamwork.

Later on, I shall discuss this heterogeneity. But let me give a single example of unanticipated developments immediately. The volume *Australians 1838* was in effect, bid for, some time on, by two young historians then in Perth, Alan Atkinson and Marian Aveling: their bid was eventually successful. They had been excited by the prospect which Ken Inglis had opened up when he visited Western Australia during his 1977 tour; they felt that it offered much hope for the sort of history that appealed to their generation. They were deeply interested in the possibilities of the new 'history from below', fervently anti-authoritarian by instinct, and much attracted by collective forms of work. In fact, they set up an *1838* collective in 1980, open to everyone who contributed anything to the journal for 1838 studies which they had established, with the wryly pointed title, *The push from the bush*. This ethos and this *modus operandi* were maintained throughout the composition of their book, with much consultation, exchange of drafts, conferences and co-operative writing. Most of the chapters ended up with several authors, one with no fewer than eight contributors, all loyal to the collective's initial resolution (I quote from the volume's introduction) 'to present the minds of people living in Australia in 1838 as far as possible from inside, by recounting the language and behaviour of day-to-day situations . . . going *beyond* the records of the elite so as to recreate the minds of the inarticulate and powerless'. I think readers will agree that Atkinson and Aveling have succeeded brilliantly in their purpose.

The second benefit of the douches of cold and tepid water with which we were showered in 1977 was that they confirmed the importance of devolving as much of the project as possible to other universities, and throughout the country. This was not—could not have been—as much a matter of strategic planning as of seizing opportunities as they arose. And in fact the requisite opportunities appeared. The obvious centre for *1838*, in its early years, was Perth. The ideal editors for *1888* emerged in Melbourne, and for *1938* in Adelaide and Sydney. The most important devolution of all was the appointment of Frank Crowley as general editor of the whole series of reference volumes, now termed Section B. Not only did this create another headquarters (or at least sub-headquarters) in Sydney but also it meant that Crowley's university, New South Wales, would henceforth support the project financially, on a very considerable scale. Of course, this successful dispersion of the undertaking owed much to luck; but I should like to think that the Founding Fathers of Canberra did something to help luck along, or at least that they recognised her when they met her in the street.

So—we were democratised and judiciously scattered about the continent long before anyone had put pen to paper. But I should also make it clear that three centralising and controlling elements were retained: not for nothing had I served, however humbly, on the *New history of Ireland*. First, the ultimate authority, the Management Committee, remained substantially in the hands of our History department in Canberra: the head of department was chairman *ex officio*. Secondly, we set absolute deadlines, not only for completion but also for each major stage in the production: we were, in one sense (though only one!), fortunate in having a ready-made date by which, come hell or highwater, the books would have to appear before the public. And thirdly, we decided to use the various production stages as tests for the punctuality of our contributors and to eliminate all who failed to produce whatever was required by the specified time, and to search for replacements as soon as the malingerers (however eminent) were identified and disposed of. I cannot claim that we quite lived up to this stern resolution, but we certainly went a fair way down the audacious path.

On 28 March 1978 the interim Management Committee wound itself up, and the Management Committee proper took its place. By now, general editors—Inglis and Crowley—had been appointed for sections A and B respectively, as well as convenors (who were really proto-editors) for *1788*, *1838*, *1888* and *1938*. Besides, the ANU had appointed a special assistant general editor for Section A, and the UNSW a similar officer for Section B: these were full-time appointments, essentially managerial and executive in design.

All these people, with some later additions, constituted a newly formed Editorial Board, which would govern the content, style and method of the books, independently. The general title *Australians* was proposed by Bill Gammage at an early meeting of this board and accepted at once as a simple inspiration. Meanwhile a fifth volume, *Australians from 1939*, had been added to Section A; and although the *Atlas* and the *Guide to sources* and *Historical statistics* had been confirmed in Section B, its fourth volume, the *Handbook*, was to remain an uncertainty. Eventually it was partitioned into a *Historical dictionary* and the chronology-cum-gazetteer *Events and places*, the latter an unanticipated addition to the collection. Final decisions on editors, contributors and all else were due to be made by 1981, but in the interim the working parties for each volume would be laying the foundations with an eye to completion by 1985 and 1986.

In short, we had hit ourselves over the head with a bottle of champagne, glided down the slipway, and recruited many of the artificers who would labour in the still-empty hull.

For a fair while we counted on public funding, and we lived from hand to mouth for the day when the Australian Bicentennial Authority would be constituted. When the authority was at last set up in 1980, we lived for the day when it would receive federal monies for distribution. Then we lived for the day when the authority would determine its support policies and its criteria for patronage. Then—we simply ran out of days. Meanwhile, universities, in particular the ANU and University of New South Wales, kept us alive from year to year, diverting to us scraps of savings and pieces of unfilled posts. The Division of National Mapping, a federal government agency, helped us generously in the creation of the *Atlas*. The Australian Research Grants Committee gave indispensable grants towards the making of particular volumes. Finally, we received cash transfusions from our publishers in the form of advances on royalties.

In our early days we had discussed publishers in a more or less desultory way, not thinking the matter urgent and assuming that we would be sure to find a victim or band of victims. But when in 1980 we invited tenders and received submissions, it became clear that the scale, technical sophistication, unknown market prospects and concentrated publication program daunted most Australian publishers. At this point Inglis happened to meet Kevin Weldon, an entrepreneur who published high quality books for the mass market. Weldon was immediately seized by the idea of our national scheme. So it was no surprise that he responded with great enthusiasm when approached by the David Syme group, publishers of the Melbourne *Age*, and John Fairfax & Sons, publishers of the *Sydney Morning Herald*, to co-publish *Australians: a historical library*. Weldon's interest proved the turning point. We were about to enter a bigger league than we had originally contemplated.

We were now History Project Incorporated, so constituted as a legal entity under the Australian Capital Territory Associations Incorporation Ordinance. I shall pass quickly over the protracted courtship and early lovers' quarrels between HPI and FSW, as the new partnership of Fairfax, Syme and Weldon came to be known. In 1982, the contract between us was finally signed and we were a married couple—at least in the sense in which Robert Louis Stevenson defined marriage, as a sort of friendship recognised by the police.

The project had been originally expected to emerge as a conventional type of multivolume academic publication, such as the *Oxford history of England* or the *New Cambridge modern history*. It is true that we had hoped, from the beginning, to write for a more general public than such series were aimed at. It was also true that—partly for this reason and partly because the book of the future would (we thought) contain much more than the printed word—we intended that the volumes should be (I quote again from early minutes) 'richly illustrated'. But FSW's vision of potential sales for the series, so much grander than any other publisher we had spoken with, provoked us to bolder thinking about both words and pictures.

It became imperative that the volumes should be written in plain (which is far from meaning inelegant) English, and as free as practicable from the argot and jargon of the various disciplines which the project would embrace. Later, Alan

Gilbert, who joined Inglis as general editor of Section A late in 1981, made this a special study. Drawing particularly upon American syntactical and grammatical research, he prepared a paper of great interest and importance for contributors, Effective presentation was another corollary of aiming at a mass market. It quickly became clear that FSW contemplated illustration upon a scale, and of a degree of sophistication, far beyond what we had had originally in mind. Our volumes have ended up with some three thousand illustrations, most of them in colour: the ratio of illustration to text is roughly one to three. Moreover, illustration was not treated as mere decoration. It was carefully interwoven with text wherever possible. These changes of emphasis added enormously to our load, and did much to make our relationship with the publisher both more complex and more intimate than we had imagined. FSW set up editorial and design systems from the start, so that from 1982 on we were working not in a vacuum but in continuous communication with our partner. At last, in November 1986, arrived the joint meeting at which we could all leaf through the first two finished books, artefacts of our common purpose.

In the heady days in 1976 and 1977 we imagined that we would end in some immense thunderclap of achievement. Instead, we have seemed to dwindle gradually into annihilation. Exhaustion has overlaid and smothered jubilation. In W. B. Yeats's words:

> Too long a sacrifice
> Can make a stone of the heart.

Was it all worth while? Were those critics right who argued at the start that such a prodigious mustering and spending of intellectual resources was a mistaken, indeed a most wasteful strategy?

I can answer only for myself. I see many reasons for concluding that the game has after all been worth the candle; and I shall offer the five which seem to me most powerful.

First, in the reference books, deep foundations have been laid for Australian historiography in general. Virtually *de novo*, the project has created a series of historical statistics, a historical chronology and gazetteer, a historical atlas, a historical dictionary and a major guide to sources. This was achieved under the general editorship of Frank Crowley to 1985, and of Peter Spearritt from 1985 to the finishing line. No-one would pretend to perfection or finality for any of these volumes or part-volumes. But at least a solid basis has been laid over the entire range of reference works.

Secondly, the project has, I believe, integrated Aboriginal with what we may loosely term European Australian history, as never before. The planned *1788* ended up as *To 1788*, with four-fifths of its content devoted to pre-European Australia. This brilliant survey of the Aboriginal era, itself a *tour de force*, is thoroughly knit into the doom of traditional Aboriginal life, as signalled by the arrival of the British fleet in 1788. In addition—and of no less importance, I should say—each of the volumes set in later years takes up other Aboriginal themes and interweaves them with the expansion of white Australia. Again, the historiographical map seems to have been changed significantly. Already, the old virtually automatic identification of Australian history with the settlements of the past two centuries looks *passé*. The project itself has fiercely eschewed the celebratory note: 1988 is treated throughout as the anniversary of a revolutionary happening, not as the starting point of a neo-whig interpretation, or glorification, of a short stretch of time.

Thirdly, the project has had a striking effect upon the historical profession in Australia. It is even arguable that it created this profession, in the sense that the enterprise has forced a multitude of Australian historians into collective activity and co-operative interaction upon a hitherto undreamt-of scale. There were working parties of up to thirty people on particular volumes and constant traffic between one volume and another: commonly, the interchanges proceeded for several years. Paradoxically, the inevitable—indeed desirable—differences in historical presuppositions and general philosophy had—all in all—a centripetal rather than a centrifugal effect upon the participants. The *esprit de corps* growing out of the common commitment tended to bring a corps itself into being, over time. Moreover, by a further paradox, the historians themselves have been not only enriched but also stung into a greater self-awareness, by all the close and constant work with people from other disciplines, which the project practically enjoined. Among these disciplines, I would stress particularly geography and anthropology, as well as prehistory and economic history. In short, it seems to me that history in Australia has emerged from the experience immensely strengthened, structurally as well as intellectually.

Fourthly, the project dragged at least those of us who needed to be dragged into the late twentieth century. In saying this, I refer, in part, to our technical education. Without the word processor and the disc our task would have been impossible. Our colour and design requirements called for the newest processes. All this experience of modern publishing has filtered downwards. Even if only at second or third hand, our academics should have received useful glimpses of the future.

This is perhaps also true of some more fundamental matters. As we have seen the project's objective has been to reach a very wide and varied public without the sacrifice of any principle of scholarship. This high ambition did not stop at windy rhetoric and exhortation. Gilbert's work on words reached and—we trust— exercised some degree of influence, small or great, upon our hundreds of contributors. Correspondingly, the systematic collection of non-literary forms of evidence, and the attempt to render text and illustration mutually supporting and cross-reflective, have surely made an enduring impression on our trade.

Few words have been more overworked by historians during the past twenty years than 'modernisation'. But rarely if ever do we think of it in relation to ourselves. Yet the mechanics of composition, the economics of publishing and the potentiality of readership—not to add, listenership and spectatorship—have been changing rapidly and profoundly. I do not want to exaggerate the importance of the *forms* of communication. The substance of what is to be communicated is, and always will be, absolutely paramount. Nonetheless, we should know what we are about in the times in which we write; and the project has proved a technical school, or forcing-house, for many of the rising as well as the declining generation of Australian historians.

The fifth, final and (to my mind) most important reverberations of the project will, I believe, follow from the slice approach. The exclusive study of a single year is not of course without precedent. At least one distinguished book is based upon this method, and the *New history of Ireland* itself employs it. But never has it been attempted on such a scale, or by such large numbers of historians, or with such single-minded rigour. I think that one can fairly claim that, as deployed in *Australians: a historical library*, it is a truly revolutionary device.

Each volume group interpreted its task, and dealt with its cross-sectional layer, in a different fashion. *Australians from 1939* was practically by definition barred from slicing its half-century assignment, although its editors were also to eschew conventional narrative structures. But all the other books took individual approaches. *To 1788*, charged with 40 000 years of pre-white Australian history, could obviously not adhere to slicing proper. Even so, it was deeply influenced by the general method. In the final portion of the book, 'Sydney 1788' lent itself to and duly received an orthodox cross-sectional treatment. But what is really interesting is the manner in which much of the remainder of *To 1788* is shaped or coloured by the principle of slicing, as authors depict Aboriginal life in an actual or metaphorical 1788—the eve of European settlement whenever that moment happened in different parts of the continent.

Australians 1838 was, as I have said, the most closely collaborative volume of all. Like coalmining, history from below lent itself to collective effort. The book has taken, as its introduction proclaims, 'a critical stance towards the social values of the past', and tried to reconstruct the Australia of its particular year in terms of so-called ordinary events in the lives of so-called ordinary people, their weddings, church-going, funerals, groupings, legal and business dealings and the like. The very roll-call of titles of the middle chapters of *1838*—Families, Work, Markets, Meetings, People confined—is practically a manifesto of the history of the unsung and long-forgotten—men, women and children, too.

The *1888* volume was *organised* upon more conventional lines, and subject to more authoritative editorial direction, than any of the others. The editors selected their own team of contributors and drove them systematically through exchanges of drafts and discussion meetings. Yet their interpretation of the slices was far from commonplace. One of the editors, Graeme Davison, has noted the influence of French historiography as embodied in the journal *Annales*. He observes of *1888*:

> insofar as we have a specific model it is perhaps the kind of fully textured detailed portrait of environment, economy, society and politics that one finds in Fernand Braudel's *The Mediterranean and the Mediterranean world in the age of Philip II*. We aim to portray, more fully than hitherto, the regional and social diversity of Australia in 1888 and the ways in which different environments and regional economies were mediated in family structures and class relations.

Moreover, the *1888* editors were bold in selecting chapter topics. These were often quite out of the ordinary; Distance, Death, Capitals and Energy are examples. In fact, the Energy chapter provides an excellent illustration of what the slice approach can yield. In conventional narrative historiography the emphasis would almost certainly be placed upon the extraordinary growth in the newer forms of energy, coal, oil and electricity, during the 1880s. This is the normal patterning of the narrative. But the slice view, across the entire spectrum and at a fixed point in time, shows that horse power, in the ancient and literal sense, still easily predominated in the Australia of 1888; that the next most important source of energy was the oldest of all, human muscle; and that the rate of innovation varied widely from region to region and between the various sectors of the economy. Energy, in another sense, might well be taken as the emblem of this volume. One emerges—or at least I emerged—from reading it, dazzled by the new perspectives and tingling with intellectual excitement or liberation.

The *1938* editors took as their starting point the fact that the year itself was within the living memory of many Australians. One of the basic resources developed immediately was a collection of interviews with a sample of people who were growing up during the 1930s. In all, nearly four hundred interviews were taped. In length they varied from 45 minutes to nine hours, and they concentrated so far as practicable on the year to which the volume was dedicated. In a sense therefore it was *recollection* itself which was sliced in this particular exercise. The immediate value of the interviews in the composition of the book varied of course from topic to topic, and according to author's inclination. But they have also a lasting value as a source, which quite transcends the specific purpose for which they were assembled. *Australians 1938* was also able to apply the slice precisely in its section entitled 'Pioneers on parade', which deals with the Australian sesquicentennial celebrations and anti-celebrations. In neither case—one profoundly hopes—do they constitute a dress rehearsal for 1988, but are rather two flies in amber fixed forever in their antique confrontation.

Even this lightning sketch should have made clear that the slice, as deployed in these books, is not a formula, not a new scholasticism, not an orthodoxy, not even a taking of sides in any great methodological debate. Its makers do not assert that the slice is the only, or the best, or even an always practicable or an always desirable mode of composing history. They accept that in Clio's, as well as in a more transcendental house, there are many mansions. They even refrain from throwing the occasional ideological brick—deliberately, at least—into any other dwelling. But, I would argue, the method has its own special value, which renders it the crown and glory of our project. I know of no more eloquent or telling elaboration of this claim than that put forward by Davison in his paper, 'Slicing Australian history'. 'In constructing his narrative', he writes,

> the historian has the immense advantage of hindsight: he selects those facts or events which appear to favour that known outcome and he ignores those which are irrelevant to it, whether or not they seemed important to contemporaries. By focusing upon an arbitrarily chosen moment of time the slice approach acts as a corrective to the inbuilt teleological bias of narrative history. It implies that we *temporarily* abstain from the search for 'the most significant years, or the busiest or the epochal' and concentrate instead upon the routine, the ordinary and mundane. Instead of assigning significance to events in terms of a known outcome or *telos* it gently subverts the 'received notions of the rhythms or contours of Australian history'. Instead of exalting the established heroes of Australian history, it aims to rescue the struggling selector, the suburban housewife, even perhaps the landboomer's clerk, from the 'appalling condescension of posterity'.

But it would be quite out of kilter with the project to end on too celebratory or even congratulatory a note. Our authors tend to see the project as a living thing, not a dead achievement, a seeding rather than a harvest cut and garnered. Nonetheless, I, who have neither written nor edited a line in any of the volumes, may perhaps be allowed to boast on behalf of the many who spent years in this grinding work, now completed in good time to help readers throughout and beyond Australia to understand the experience of humanity in this continent from its beginnings to 1988.

%	per cent	AIIA	Australian Institute of International Affairs	*Aust geog stud*	*Australian geographical studies*
£	pound(s)	AIM	Australian Inland Mission		
A & R	Angus & Robertson, Publishers, Sydney	AIS	Australian Iron and Steel	*Aust j polit & hist*	*Australian journal of politics and history*
AA	Australian Archives	AJCP	Australian Joint Copying Project		
AACOBS	Australian Advisory Council on Bibliographic Services	AK	Knight of the Order of Australia	AWA	Amalgamated Wireless (Australasia) Ltd
AA Co	Australian Agricultural Company	ALCOA	Aluminium Company of Australia	AWAS	Australian Women's Army Service
AAL	Australian Aborigine League *or* Aboriginal Advancement League	ALP	Australian Labor Party	AWGC	Australian Woolgrowers Council
		AM	Member of the Order of Australia *or* amplitude modulation	AWU	Australian Workers' Union
AAP	Australian Associated Press			BA	Bachelor of Arts
AAPA	Australian Aborigines Progressive Association	AMA	Australian Medical Association	Bart	Baronet
		AMIA	Australian Meat Industries Association	BBC	British Broadcasting Corporation
ABC	Australian Broadcasting Commission (now Corporation)	AMP	Australian Mutual Provident	BE (Aero)	Bachelor of Engineering (Aerodynamics)
		AMS	Aboriginal Medical Service		
Aborig(s)	Aborigine(s), Aboriginal	AMWU	Amalgamated Metal Workers' Union	BHP	Broken Hill Proprietary Company Limited
ABS	Australian Bureau of Statistics	ANA	Australian National Airways	BIG	Basic Industry Group
AC	Companion of the Order of Australia	Anon	Anonymous	BLF	Builders' Labourers' Federation
ACER	Australian Council for Educational Research, Melbourne, Victoria	ANOP	Australian National Opinion Poll	B Litt	Bachelor of Letters
		ANU	Australian National University	BOAC	British Overseas Airways Corporation
ACF	Australian Conservation Foundation	ANUP	Australian National University Press, Canberra, ACT	Br	British
ACI	Australian Consolidated Industries	ANZAC	Australia and New Zealand Army Corps	Brev-Maj	Brevet-Major
				BrPP	British *Parliamentary Papers*
ACSPA	Australian Council of Salaried and Professional Associations	ANZUS	Australia – New Zealand – United States Treaty	Bt	Baronet
ACT	Australian Capital Territory	AO	Officer of the Order of Australia	*Bus archives & hist*	*Business archives and history*
ACTU	Australian Council of Trade Unions	AONSW	Archives Office of New South Wales		
AD	Australian Democrats	AOTas	Archives Office of Tasmania	BWIU	Building Workers' Industrial Union
ADB	*Australian Dictionary of Biography*	AP	Australia Party	*c*	*circa*
ADC	Aboriginal Development Corporation	app	appendix	°C	degrees Centigrade
add ms	additional manuscript	approx	approximately	C	Commonwealth
AEU	Amalgamated Engineering Union	ARU	Australian Railways Union	CAAMA	Central Australian Aboriginal Media Association
AFC	Australian Flying Corps *or* Australian Film Commission	ASEAN	Association of South-East Asian Nations	CAD	Commission for Aboriginal Development
		ASIC	Australian standard industrial classification	CAGEO	Council of Australian Government Employee Organisations
AFDA	Australian Funeral Directors' Association	ASIO	Australian Security Intelligence Organization		
AGPS	Australian Government Printing Service, Canberra, ACT	Assoc	Association	CAI	Confederation of Australian Industry
agric	agriculture (= al)	ATC	Air Training Corps	CBA	Commonwealth Bank of Australia
AHQ	Army Headquarters	Aust	Australia(n)		
AIDC	Australian Industry Development Corporation	Aust Agric Co	Australian Agricultural Company	CBCS	Commonwealth Bureau of Census and Statistics
AIDS	Acquired Immune Deficiency Syndrome	*Aust econ hist rev*	*Australian economic history review*	CEP	Community Employment Programme
AIF	Australian Imperial Force	*Aust 1888*	*Australia 1888*	Capt(s)	Captain(s)

CB	Companion of the Bath	**DBE**	Dame Commander of the Order of the British Empire	**FRCOG**	Fellow of the Royal College of Obstetricians and Gynaecologists
CBE	Commander of the Order of the British Empire	**DEIR**	Department of Employment and Industrial Relations	**FRCS**	Fellow of the Royal College of Surgeons
ch(s)	chapter(s)	**dept**	department	**g**	gram(s)
Cdr	Commander	**DFC**	Distinguished Flying Cross	**gals**	gallons
CH	Companion of Honour	**DGCBE**	Dame Grand Cross of the Order of the British Empire	**GBE**	Knight or Dame Grand Cross of the Order of the British Empire
CHOGM	Commonwealth Heads of Government Meeting	**discov**	discovered		
CIA	Central Intelligence Agency	**DLP**	Democratic Labor Party	**GCB**	Knight or Dame Grand Cross of the Bath
CIB	Criminal Investigation Bureau	**DM**	Deutschmark		
CIE	Companion of the Order of the Indian Empire	*DNB*	*Dictionary of National Biography*	**GCIE**	Knight Grand Commander of the Order of the Indian Empire
CIF	cost, insurance, freight	**Doc**	Document		
cm	centimetre	**DP**	displaced persons	**GCMG**	Knight or Dame Grand Cross of the Order of St Michael and St George
CM	Master of Surgery	**Dr**	Doctor		
CMF	Citizens' Military Forces	**DSC**	Distinguished Service Cross		
CMG	Companion of the Order of St Michael and St George	**DSO**	Companion of the Distinguished Service Order	**GCSI**	Knight Grand Commander of the Star of India
CMS	Church Missionary Society	**DSS**	Department of Social Security	**GCVD**	Knight or Dame Grand Cross of the Royal Victorian Order
co, Co	company, Company	*DT*	*Daily Telegraph*		
CO (followed by class and piece number)	Colonial office records in the Public Record Office, London	*Econ record*	*Economic record*	**GDP**	Gross Domestic Product
		ECT	electroconvulsive therapy	**Gen**	General
		ED	Efficiency Decoration	*GG*	*Government Gazette*
Col	Colonel	**ed(s)**	editor(s)/edited by	**GMH**	General Motors – Holden
col sec	colonial secretary	**edn**	edition	**GNP**	Gross National Product
Com	Commonwealth	**EEC**	European Economic Community	**Gov**	Governor
				Gov-gen	Governor-general
Com bur met bull	*Commonwealth bureau of meteorology bulletin*	**EPA**	Environment Protection Authority	**govt**	government
				GPO	General Post Office
comp	compiler/compiled	**esp**	especially	**GW**	gigawatt
Corp	Corporation	**est**	estimated	**GWh**	gigawatthour
CP/CPA	Communist Party of Australia	**estab**	established	**ha**	hectare(s)
CPI	Consumer Price Index	*et al*	*and others*	**H of C**	British House of Commons
CPSU	Communist Party of the Soviet Union	**EVAO**	Estimated Value of Agricultural Operations	*Hist stud*	*Historical studies*
CRA	Conzinc Riotinto of Australia Limited	**EYL**	Eureka Youth League	**HO** (followed by class and piece number)	Home Office records in the Public Record Office, London
		facs	facsimile		
CSIRO	Commonwealth Scientific and Industrial Research Organization	**FCAA**	Federal Council for the Advancement of Aborigines		
CSO	Colonial Secretary's Office	**FCAATSI**	Federal Council for the Advancement of Aborigines and Torres Strait Islanders	**HQ**	headquarters
CSR	Colonial Sugar Refining Company Limited			**hr**	hour
				HRA	*Historical Records of Australia,*
CUP	Cambridge University Press, Melbourne, Vic. CUP publications issued in Cambridge are shown as Cambridge, CUP	**f (ff)**	folio (folios) *or* following page(s)	*HRNSW*	*Historical Records of New South Wales*
		FHP	Family History Project, University of Melbourne Archives	*HRV*	*Historical Records of Victoria*
		FIA	Federated Ironworkers' Association	**IAC**	Industries Assistance Commission
CVO	Companion of the Royal Victorian Order	**fig**	figure	*ibid*	in the same work
CYB	*Commonwealth year book*	**FM**	Frequency modulation	**IBM**	International Business Machines
d	defeated	**FOB**	free on board	**Inst**	Institute
d	penny/pence	**Fr**	Father	**IPEC**	Interstate Parcel Express Company
DAA	Department of Aboriginal Affairs	**FRAeS**	Fellow of the Royal Aeronautical Society	**IRO**	International Refugee Organisation

Is	Island	MCG	Melbourne Cricket Ground	NSW	New South Wales
IUP	Irish University Press, Dublin, Ireland	MD	Doctor of Medicine	NSWC	New South Wales Coalition
		mfm	microfilm	NT	Northern Territory
IWW	International Workers of the World	mg	milligram(s)	NTFL	Northern Territory Football League
J	Journal	MGP	Morgan Gallup Poll	NY	New York
J Aust hist soc	*Journal of the Australian historical society*	MHR	Member of the House of Representatives	NZ	New Zealand
		MIA	Murrumbidgee Irrigation Area	OBE	Officer of the Order of the British Empire
J Aust Stud	*Journal of Australian studies*	MIM	Mount Isa Mines Company	OECD	Organization for Economic Cooperation and Development
JP	Justice of the Peace	MJA	*Medical Journal of Australia*		
jr	junior	ML	Mitchell Library		
J R Aust Hist Soc	*Journal of the Royal Australian Historical Society*	MLA	Member of the Legislative Assembly	OHC	Oral History Collection, Faculty of Education, Monash University
KBE	Knight Commander of the Order of the British Empire	MLC	Member of the Legislative Council		
		M Litt	Master of Letters	OHP	Oral History Project, Department of Politics, Macquarie University
KC	King's Counsel	MP	Member of Parliament		
KCB	Knight Commander of the Order of the Bath	ms(s)	manuscript(s)	OPEC	Organization of Petroleum Exporting Countries
		MS	Master of Surgery; Master of Science (USA)		
KCMG	Knight Commander of the Order of St Michael and St George			OTC	Overseas Telecommunications Commission
		MTEA	Metal Trades Employers' Association	OUP	Oxford University Press, Melbourne. OUP publications issued in London are shown as London, OUP
KCVO	Knight Commander of the Royal Victorian Order	MTIA	Metal Trades Industry Association of Australia		
KG	Knight of the Garter	Mt(s)	Mount (Mountains)		
KH	Knight of Hanover	MUP	Melbourne University Press, Parkville, Victoria	p	page
km	kilometre(s)			P & C	Parents and Citizens Association
km/h	kilometres per hour			P & O	The Peninsula and Oriental Steam Navigation Company
KP	Knight of St Patrick	MVO	Member Royal Victorian Order		
KSTJ	Knight of the Order of St John of Jerusalem	n	note	PC	Privy Councillor
		na	not available	*PD*	*Parliamentary Debates* (followed by volume, year and page number)
KT	Knight of the Thistle	NAC	National Aboriginal Conference		
Labour hist	*Labour history*	NACC	National Aboriginal Consultative Committee		
La TL	La Trobe Library			PhD	Doctor of Philosophy
lb(s)	pound(s)	NAOU	North Australia Observer Unit	PIB	Papuan Infantry Battalion
LBSA	Library Board of South Australia	NASA	National Aeronautical and Space Administration	PJ	petajoule
LC	Legislative Council			Pl	Place
Lieut	Lieutenant	Nat Pk (s)	National Park (s)	PMG	Postmaster General
Lieut-Col	Lieutenant-Colonel	Nat T	National Trust	pm pa	per million per annum
Lieut-Gen	Lieutenant-General	NAWU	North Australian Workers Union	PNG	Papua New Guinea
Lieut-Gov	Lieutenant-Governor			popn	population
LLB	Bachelor of Laws	NCC	National Civic Council	POW	Prisoner(s) of War
L-NP	Liberal-National Party	nd	no date	*PP*	*Parliamentary Papers* (followed by volume, year and page number)
m	metre(s)	NEF	New Education Fellowship		
m/mill	million	NFF	National Farmers' Federation		
M³	cubic metre(s)	NGWO(s)	Non-government welfare organization(s)	pprs	papers
MA	Master of Arts			PRO	Public Record Office, London
Maj	Major			pseud	pseudonym
Maj-Gen	Major-General	NH & MRC	National Health and Medical Research Council	PT	Point *or* Port
MB	Bachelor of Medicine			*Push*	*Push from the bush*
MBE	Member of the Order of the British Empire	NIDA	National Institute of Dramatic Art, Sydney	QC	Queen's Counsel
				Qld	Queensland
		NLA	National Library of Australia	R	River
		no(s)	number(s)	Ra	Range
MC	Military Cross	NRMA	National Roads and Motorists' Association of New South Wales	RAAF	Royal Australian Air Force
				RAF	Royal Air Force

RAN	Royal Australian Navy	**sq km**	square kilometre(s)	**UQP**	University of Queensland Press, St Lucia, Qld
RBA	Reserve Bank of Australia	**Sr**	Sister	**US/USA**	United States of America
RBT	random breath testing	**SRC**	Swan River Colony	**USSR**	Union of Soviet Socialist Republics
Rd	Road	**SRD**	statutory reserve deposit		
repr	reprint (ed)	**St**	Street *or* Saint	**UWAP**	University of Western Australia Press, Nedlands, WA
rev	revised	**STD**	Subscriber Trunk Dialling		
Rev	Reverend	**SUP**	Sydney University Press, Sydney, NSW	**v**	versus
Rm	Reichsmark			**V&P**	Votes and Proceedings
RN	Royal Navy	**supp**	supplementary	**VC**	Victoria Cross
RNE	Register of the National Estate	**Supt**	Superintendent	**VDC**	Volunteer Defence Corps
Roy Comm	Royal Commission	**TAA**	Trans-Australia Airlines	**VDL**	Van Diemen's Land
		TAB	Totalisator Agency Board	**VFA**	Victorian Football Association
RSI	repetition strain injury	**Tas**	Tasmania	**VFL**	Victorian Football League
RSL	Returned Services League	**TB**	Tuberculosis	**Vic**	Victoria
rlwy(s)	railway(s)	**Tb(s)**	table(s)	**vol(s)**	volume(s)
s	shilling(s)	**Tce**	Terrace	**VSL**	Victorian State Library
SA	South Australia	*TCJ*	*Town and Country Journal*	**WA**	Western Australia
SAA	South Australian Archives	**TLC**	Trades and Labour Council	**WAAAF**	Women's Auxiliary Australian Air Force
SANFL	South Australian National Football League	**ThD**	Doctor of Theology		
		TNT	Thomas Nationwide Transport	**WEA**	Workers Educational Association
SBS	Special Broadcasting Service	**trans**	translator/translated by	**WEB**	Women's Employment Board
SCEGGS	Sydney Church of England Girls' Grammar School	**TWU**	Transport Workers' Union	**WEL**	Women's Electoral Lobby
		UAP	United Australia Party	**WPI**	wholesale price index
SCG	Sydney Cricket Ground	**UK**	United Kingdom	**WRANS**	Women's Royal Australian Naval Service
SEATO	South East Asia Treaty Organization	**UN**	United Nations		
		uncat	uncatalogued	**WWF**	Waterside Workers Federation
SG	*Sydney Gazette*	**UNE**	University of New England	**YCL**	Young Communist League
SH	*Sydney Herald*	**UNESCO**	United Nations Educational, Scientific and Cultural Organization	**YMCA**	Young Men's Christian Association
SLSA	State Library of South Australia				
SMH	*Sydney Morning Herald*			**YWCA**	Young Women's Christian Association
Soc	Society	**UNSWP**	University of New South Wales Press, Kensington, NSW		
sp	species *or* starting price			**yr(s)**	year(s)

'Arts funding fiasco', by Michael Fitzjames. Government
funding of the arts has often come under considerable debate.
Some believe that occupations such as writing should be
labours of love, and that organisations such as the Australian
Opera should be run on a commercial basis with productions
being wholly funded through ticket sales and commercial
sponsorships. Pen and ink. First published in the
National Times, 1986.

JOHN FAIRFAX & SONS

I
THE ARTS

AGE BOOK OF THE YEAR

Two awards annually, one for imaginative writing and one for non-fiction, judged to be of outstanding literary merit and expressing Australia's identity.

YEAR	AUTHOR	TITLE
1974	David Foster	*The pure land*
	C. M. H. Clark	*A history of Australia*, vol 3
1975	Thea Astley	*A kindness cup*
1976	A. D. Hope	*A late picking*
	Hugh Stretton	*Capitalism, socialism and the environment*
1977	Graham Freudenberg	*A certain grandeur*
1978	Christopher Koch	*The year of living dangerously*
	Patsy Adam-Smith	*The Anzacs*
1979	Roger McDonald	*1915*
1980	David Ireland	*A woman of the future*
	Murray Bail	*Homesickness*
1981	Eric Rolls	*A million wild acres*
	Blanche d'Alpuget	*Turtle beach*
1982	David Malouf	*Fly away Peter*
	Geoffrey Serle	*John Monash: a biography*
1983	Elizabeth Jolley	*Mr Scobie's riddle*
	Lloyd Robson	*A history of Tasmania*
1984	Nicholas Hasluck	*The Bellarmine jug*
	John Rickard	*H. B. Higgins: the rebel as judge*
1985	Peter Carey	*Illywhacker*
	Chester Eagle	*Mapping the paddocks*
	Hugh Lunn	*Vietnam: a reporter's war*
1986	Joan London	*Sister ships*
	Gary Kinnane	*George Johnston; a biography*

ALAN MARSHALL AWARD

Awarded annually by the Fellowship of Australian Writers for a manuscript containing a strong narrative element (novel, collection of stories, or long narrative poem).

YEAR	AUTHOR	YEAR	AUTHOR
1976	Geoff Taylor	1982	Gary Langford
1977	Lee Harding	1983	Eleanor Graeme-Evans
1978	Maria Lewitt		
1979	Serge Liberman	1984	Serge Liberman
1980	Serge Liberman	1985	Garry Hurle
1981	Beverley Farmer	1986	Jenny Herrera

AUSTRALIAN CHILDREN'S BOOK OF THE YEAR

Awarded annually by the Australian Children's Book Council.

YEAR	AUTHOR	TITLE
1946	Leslie Rees	*Karrawingi the emu*
1947	Not awarded	
1948	Frank Hurley	*Shackleton's argonauts*
1949	Alan Villiers	*Whalers of the midnight sun*
1950	Not awarded	
1951	Ruth C. Williams	*Verity of Sydney Town*
1952	Eve Pownall	*The Australia book*
1953	John Phipson	*Good luck to the rider*
	J. H. & W. D. Martin	*Aircraft of today and tomorrow*
1954	K. Langloh Parker	*Australian legendary tales* (selected by Henrietta Drake-Brockman)

AUSTRALIAN CHILDREN'S BOOK OF THE YEAR continued

YEAR	AUTHOR	TITLE
1955	Norman B. Tindale & H. A. Lindsay	*The first walkabout*
1956	Patricia Wrightson	*The crooked snake*
	Peggy Barnard	*Wish and the magic nut*
1957	Enid Moodie Heddle (ed)	*The boomerang book of legendary tales*
1958	Nan Chauncy	*Tiger in the bush*
1959	Nan Chauncy	*Devil's hill*
	John Gunn	*Sea menace*
1960	Kylie Tennant	*All the proud tribesmen*
1961	Nan Chauncy	*Tangara*
1962	L. H. Evers	*The Racketty Street gang*
	Joan Woodberry	*Rafferty rides a winner*
1963	Joan Phipson	*The family conspiracy*
1964	Eleanor Spence	*The green laurel*
1965	H. F. Brinsmead	*Pastures of the blue crane*
1966	Ivan Southall	*Ash Road*
1967	Mavis Thorpe Clarke	*The Min-Min*
1968	Ivan Southall	*To the wild sky*
1969	Margaret Balderson	*When jays fly to Barbmo*
1970	Annette Macarthur Onslow	*Uhu*
1971	Ivan Southall	*Bread and honey*
1972	Hesba Brinsmead	*Longtime passing*
1973	Noreen Shelley	*Family at the lookout*
1974	Patricia Wrightson	*The Nargun and the stars*
1975	Not awarded	
1976	Ivan Southall	*Fly west*
1977	Eleanor Spence	*The October child*
1978	Patricia Wrightson	*The ice is coming*
1979	Ruth Manley	*The plum-rain scroll*
1980	Lee Harding	*Displaced person*
1981	Ruth Park	*Playing Beatie Bow*
1982	Colin Thiele	*The valley between*
1983	Victor Kelleher	*Master of the grove*

FELLOWSHIP OF AUSTRALIAN WRITERS BARBARA RAMSDEN AWARD

Awarded annually to the author and publisher's editor of an Australian book of quality.

YEAR	AUTHOR	TITLE	PUBLISHER'S EDITOR
1971	Michael Cannon	*Who's master? Who's man?*	Sue Ebury
1972	J. A. La Nauze	*The making of the Australian Constitution*	Janet Mackenzie
1973	C. M. H. Clark	*A history of Australia*, vol 3	Carol Bram
	Dorothy Green	*Ulysses bound: Henry Handel Richardson and her fiction*	Shirley Purchase
1974	David Foster	*The pure land*	Lee White
	John Levi and G. F. J. Bergman	*Australian genesis: Jewish convicts and settlers 1788–1850*	Michael Page
	Ronald McKie	*The mango tree*	Robert Roseman

BARBARA RAMSDEN AWARD continued

1975	Geoffrey Blainey	*Triumph of the nomads*	Lee White
	Thomas Keneally	*Gossip from the forest*	Philip Ziegler
	Mary Rose Liverani	*The winter sparrows*	Sue Ebury
1976	Harry Gordon	*An eyewitness history of Australia*	Jennifer Cunningham
1977	A. T. Yarwood	*Samuel Marsden: the great survivor*	Carol Bram
1978	C. M. H. Clark	*A history of Australia,* vol 4	Carol Bram
1979	O. H. K. Spate	*The Spanish Lake*	Patricia Croft
1980	A. W. Martin	*Henry Parkes: a biography*	Wendy Sutherland
1981	Gavin Souter	*Company of Heralds*	Wendy Sutherland
1982	Rodney Hall	*Just relations*	Sally Moss
1983	Lloyd Robson	*A history of Tasmania,* vol 1	John Bangsund
1984	E. M. Webster	*The moon man: a biography of Nikolai Miklouho-Maclay*	Wendy Sutherland
1985	Christina Stead	*Ocean of story*	John Curtain
	Peter Carey	*Illywhacker*	Craig Munro
1986	Elizabeth Jolley	*The well*	Kay Ronai

FELLOWSHIP OF AUSTRALIAN WRITERS
CHRISTOPHER BRENNAN AWARD

Formerly the FAW Robert Frost Award. Awarded to a poet whose work achieves distinction, particularly for sustained work.

YEAR	AUTHOR	YEAR	AUTHOR
1973	Robert D. FitzGerald	1979	David Campbell (posthumous)
1974	Judith Wright	1980	John Blight
1975	A. D. Hope	1981	Vincent Buckley
1976	Douglas Stewart	1982	Bruce Beaver
	James McAuley (posthumous)	1983	Bruce Dawe
	Francis Webb	1984	Les A. Murray
1977	Gwen Harwood	1985	William Hart-Smith
1978	Rosemary Dobson	1986	Peter Porter

FELLOWSHIP OF AUSTRALIAN WRITERS
C. J. DENNIS AWARD

Awarded annually by the Fellowship of Australian Writers, and funded by the Victorian Government, for a work on an Australian subject which varies from year to year.

YEAR	AUTHOR	TITLE
1976	Barbara York Main	*Spiders*
1977	Douglas Dorward	*Wild Australia*
1978	Robert F. Zacharin	*Emigrant eucalypts: gum trees as exotics*
1979	Densey Clyne	*The garden jungle*

C.J. DENNIS AWARD continued

1980	Graham Pizzey	*A field guide to the birds of Australia*
1981	Eric Rolls	*A million wild acres*
1982	Densey Clyne	*Wildlife in the suburbs*
1983	Michael and Irene Morecombe	*Discovering Australia's national parks and naturelands*
1984	C. M. Finney	*To sail beyond the sunset: natural history in Australia 1699–1829*
1985	John Landy	*Close to nature*
1986	Ann Moyal	*A bright and savage land*

FELLOWSHIP OF AUSTRALIAN WRITERS
HERB THOMAS LITERARY AWARD
(Formerly Con Weickhardt Award)

Awarded annually by the Fellowship of Australian Writers until 1975 for the manuscript of a novel by a previously unpublished novelist, and since then for a published work of biography, autobiography or memoirs.

YEAR	AUTHOR	TITLE
1973	Kris Hemensley and Gordon Graham	
1974	John Durack and Elizabeth Jolley	
1975	Niall Brennan	
1976	Harry Marks	*I can jump oceans*
1977	Lennard Bickel	*This accursed land*
	A. T. Yarwood	*Samuel Marsden: the great survivor*
1978	Ray Ericksen	*Ernest Giles – explorer and traveller, 1835–1897*
	John Kerr	*Matters for judgement*
1979	Donald Horne	*In search of Billy Hughes*
1980	E. M. Webster	*Whirlwinds in the plain: Ludwig Leichhardt – friends, foes and history*
1981	Edward Kynaston	*A man on edge*
1982	Geoffrey Serle	*John Monash: a biography*
1983	Douglas Stewart	*Springtime in Taranaki*
1984	Craig Munro	*Wild man of letters*
1985	D. W. A. Baker	*Days of wrath: a life of John Dunmore Lang*
	D. J. Mulvaney and J. H. Calaby	*So much that is new: Baldwin Spencer 1860–1929*
1986	T. P. Boland	*James Duhig*

FELLOWSHIP OF AUSTRALIAN WRITERS
JOHN SHAW NEILSON POETRY AWARD

Awarded annually for a poem of literary merit of 14 lines or more.

YEAR	AUTHOR	YEAR	AUTHOR
1971	Alan Maxwell	1980	Jean Kent
1972	Barbara Giles	1981	Mark O'Connor
1973	Daphne Olive	1982	Vera Urban
1974	Alan Alexander	1983	Mary Dadswell
1975	Marion King	1984	Frank McMahon
1976	Kevin Hart	1985	Kevin Murray
1977	Frank McMahon	1986	Jennifer Woodhouse
1978	Anne Odgers		
1979	Paul Hutchison		

FELLOWSHIP OF AUSTRALIAN WRITERS AUSTRALIAN NATIVES' ASSOCIATION LITERATURE AWARD

Awarded annually by the Fellowship of Australian Writers for a work of sustained quality with an Australian theme.

YEAR	AUTHOR	TITLE
1978	Jessica Anderson	*Tirra Lirra by the river*
	Ronald Conway	*Land of the long weekend*
1979	David Denholm	*The colonial Australians*
1980	Frank Hardy	*Who shot George Kirkland?*
	Bill Reed	*Stigmata*
1981	Glen Tomasetti	*Man of letters*
1982	Rodney Hall	*Just relations*
1983	Laurie Clancy	*Perfect love*
1984	Roger Millis	*Serpent's tooth*
1985	John Bryson	*Evil angels*
1986	James Aldridge	*The true story of Spit Macphee*

LOCAL HISTORY AWARD

Awarded annually by the Fellowship of Australian Writers for a book of Australian local or regional history.

YEAR	AUTHOR	TITLE
1972	William Cullican and	*Fossil beach cement works,*
	John Taylor	*Mornington, Victoria*
	Mary Tuner Shaw	*Builders of Melbourne: the Cockrams and their contemporaries*
1973	Ronald Lawson	*Brisbane in the 1890s*
1974	Joan Gillison	*The colonial doctor and his town*
1975	L. E. Skinner	*Police of the pastoral frontier*
	Alan Trengrove	*'What's good for Australia!'*
1976	Bobbie Hardy	*Lament for the Barkindji*
	Willain Drage and	*Riverboats and rivermen*
	Michael Page	
1977	Hal Porter	*Bairnsdale: portrait of an Australian country town*
1978	Weston Bate	*Lucky city: the first generation at Ballarat 1851–1901*
	Graeme Davison	*The rise and fall of marvellous Melbourne*
1979	Bernard Barrett	*The civic frontier*
	C. T. Stannage	*The people of Perth*
1980	J. W. Powling	*Port Fairy – the first fifty years*
1981	Pauline Marrington	*In the sweet bye and bye*
1982	Andrew Lemon	*Broadmeadows – a forgotten history*
1983	Michael Jones	*Prolific in God's gifts*
	Andrew Lemon	*The Northcote side of the river*
1984	Janet McCalman	*Struggletown: public and private life in Richmond 1900–1965*
1985	Ken Spillman	*Identity prized: a history of Subiaco*
1986	Geoff Burrow and	*The canecutters*
	Clive Morton	

MILES FRANKLIN AWARD

Awarded annually by the trustees of the award for a published novel dealing with aspects of Australian life. If no novel submitted is judged to be of sufficient merit, a radio or television play becomes eligible.

YEAR	AUTHOR	TITLE
1957	Patrick White	*Voss*

MILES FRANKLIN AWARD continued

1958	Randolph Stow	*To the islands*
1959	Vance Palmer	*The big fellow*
1960	Elizabeth O'Connor	*The Irishman*
1961	Patrick White	*Riders in the chariot*
1962	Thea Astley	*The well dressed explorer*
	George Turner	*The cupboard under the stairs*
1963	Sumner Locke Elliot	*Careful, he might hear you*
1964	George Johnston	*My brother Jack*
1965	Thea Astley	*The slow natives*
1966	Peter Mathers	*Trap*
1967	Thomas Keneally	*Bring larks and heroes*
1968	Thomas Keneally	*Three cheers for the Paraclete*
1969	George Johnston	*Clean straw for nothing*
1970	Dal Stivens	*A horse of air*
1971	David Ireland	*The unknown industrial prisoner*
1972	Thea Astley	*The Acolyte*
1973	Not awarded	
1974	Ronald McKie	*The mango tree*
1975	Xavier Herbert	*Poor fellow my country*
1976	David Ireland	*The glass canoe*
1977	Ruth Park	*Swords and crowns and rings*
1978	Jessica Anderson	*Tirra Lirra by the river*
1979	David Ireland	*A woman of the future*
1980	Jessica Anderson	*The impersonators*
1981	Peter Carey	*Bliss*
1982	Rodney Hall	*Just relations*
1983	No award	
1984	Tim Winton	*Shallows*
1985	Christopher Koch	*The doubleman*

NATIONAL BOOK COUNCIL AWARDS FOR AUSTRALIAN LITERATURE

Two awards annually, to both author and publisher: an open award for a book judged to be of highest literary merit, and another award for a book judged to be of highest literary merit in a category other than that of the winning work.

YEAR	AUTHOR	TITLE	PUBLISHER
1974	Roland Robinson	*The drift of things*	Macmillan
	Geoffrey Serle	*From deserts the prophets come: the creative spirit in Australia, 1788–1972*	Heinemann
1975	Les Murray	*Lunch and counter lunch*	Angus & Robertson
	Laurie Clancy	*A collapsible man*	Outback Press
	William Nagle	*The odd angry shot*	Angus & Robertson
	Frank Moorhouse	*The electrical experience*	Angus & Robertson
	F. B. Vickers	*Without map or compass*	Australasian Book Society
1976	Ray Ericksen	*Cape Solitary*	Heinemann
	John Blight	*Selected poems, 1939–1975*	Nelson
1977	Harry Gordon	*An eyewitness history of Australia*	John Curry, O'Neil for Rigby

NATIONAL BOOK COUNCIL AWARDS continued

1977	Joseph Johnson	*A low breed*	Nelson
	Barry Hill	*The schools*	Penguin
1978	Helen Garner	*Monkey grip*	McPhee Gribble
	Kevin Gilbert	*Living black*	Penguin
1979	Christopher Koch	*The year of living dangerously*	Nelson
	Ray Ericksen	*Ernest Giles, explorer and traveller, 1835–1897*	Heinemann
1980	Murray Bail	*Homesickness*	Macmillan
	E. M. Webster	*Whirlwinds in the plain: Ludwig Leichhardt – friends, foes and history*	Melbourne University Press
1981	David Foster	*Moonlite*	Macmillan
	A. B. Facey	*A fortunate life*	Fremantle Arts Press
1982	Geoffrey Serle	*John Monash: a biography*	Melbourne University Press
	Peter Carey	*Bliss*	University of Queensland Press
1983	Dimitris Tsaloumas	*The observatory*	University of Queensland Press
	Olga Masters	*The home girls*	University of Queensland Press
1984	Bernard Smith	*The boy Adeodatus*	Allen Lane
	Les A. Murray	*The people's otherworld*	Angus & Robertson
1985	Peter Carey	*Illywhacker*	University of Queensland Press
	Morris Lurie	*The night we ate the sparrow*	McPhee Gribble/ Penguin
	Phillip Pepper and Tess de Araugo	*The Kurnai of Gippsland*	Hyland House
1986/7	Alan Wearne	*The nightmarkets*	Penguin

NEW SOUTH WALES PREMIER'S LITERARY AWARDS

Awarded annually in various categories.

YEAR	AUTHOR	TITLE	CATEGORY
1979	David Malouf	*An imaginary life*	Fiction
	C. M. H. Clark	*A history of Australia*, vol 4	Non-fiction
	Jenny Wagner and (illus) Ron Brooks	*John Brown, Rose and the midnight cat*	Children's
	Patricia Wrightson	*The dark bright water*	Special Children's

NSW PREMIER'S LITERARY AWARDS continued

1980	Peter Carey	*War crimes*	Fiction
	David Marr	*Barwick*	Non-fiction
	David Campbell	*Man in the honeysuckle*	Poetry (posthumous)
	Pamela Allen	*Mr Archimedes' bath*	Children's
	Catherine Berndt	*Land of the rainbow snake*	Special Children's
	Stephanie Thompson	*Australia through Italian eyes*	Ethnic
1981	Jessica Anderson	*The impersonators*	Fiction
	A. B. Facey	*A fortunate life*	Non-fiction
	Alan Gould	*Astral sea*	Poetry
	Ruth Park and (illus) Deborah Niland	*When the wind changed*	Children's
	Angelo Loukakis	*For the patriarch*	Ethnic
1982	Peter Carey	*Bliss*	Fiction
	Richard Haese	*Rebels and precursors*	Non-fiction
	Fay Zwicky	*Kaddish and other poems*	Poetry
	Nan Hunt/ Craig Smith	*Whistle up the chimney*	Children's
	Don Charlwood	*The long farewell*	Ethnic
1983	Peter Kocan	*The cure*	Fiction
	Blanche D'Alpuget	*Robert J. Hawke*	Non-fiction
	Nicholas Enright and Terence Clark	*Variations*	Play
	Vivian Smith	*Tide country*	Poetry
	Pamela Allen	*Who sank the boat?*	Children's
	Nadia Wheatley and Neil Phillips	*Five times dizzy*	Special Children's
	Spiro Zavos	*Faith of our fathers*	Ethnic
1984	Beverley Farmer	*Milk*	Fiction
	Sylvia Lawson	*The Archibald paradox*	Non-fiction
	Les A. Murray	*The people's other world*	Poetry
	Mem Fox and (illus) Julie Vivas	*Possum magic*	Children's
	Serge Liberman	*A universe of clowns*	Ethnic
	Warwick Moss	*Down an alley filled with cats*	Play
	Michael Jenkins	*Careful he might hear you*	Film writing
	Robert Caswell	*Scales of Justice*	Television writing
1985	Elizabeth Jolley	*Milk and honey*	Fiction
	Elsie Webster	*The moon man: a biography of Nikolai Miklouho-Maclay*	Non-fiction

1985	Kevin Hart	*Your shadow*	Poetry
	Nadia Wheatley	*The house that was Eureka*	Children's
	Rosa Cappiello	*Oh lucky country*	Ethnic
	Stephen Sewell	*The blind giant is dancing*	Play
	Bob Ellis and Paul Cox	*My first wife*	Film writing
	Margaret Kelly, Chris Noonan, Phillip Noyce and Russell Braddon	*The Cowra breakout*	Television writing
1986	Helen Garner	*Postcards from surfers*	Fiction
	George Munster	*A paper prince*	Non-fiction
	Phillip Pepper with Tess De Araugo	*The Kurnai of Gippsland: vol 1*	Non-fiction
	Robert Gray	*Selected poems 1963–1983*	Poetry
	James Aldridge	*The true story of Spit Macphee*	Children's
	Maria Lewitt	*No snow in December*	Ethnic
	Michael Gow	*Away*	Play
	Peter Carey and Ray Lawrence	*Bliss*	Film writing

STATE OF VICTORIA SHORT STORY AWARD

Awarded annually by the Fellowship of Australian Writers, and funded by the Victorian Government, for short stories, published or unpublished, by Australian writers.

YEAR	AUTHOR	YEAR	AUTHOR
1965	Kay Brown	1975	Iris Mulutinovic
1966	John Riviere Morris	1976	Michael Moses
1967	Geoffrey Waye	1977	James McQueen
1968	Pat Veitch	1978	James McQueen
1969	Frank Moorhouse	1979	Elizabeth Jolley
1970	Kay Brown	1980	Elizabeth Jolley
1971	Elizabeth Watson	1981	Geoffrey Dean
1972	Max Painter	1982	Tim Winton
1973	Morris Lurie	1983	Rosaleen Love
1974	Peter Knighton	1984	Chris Corbett
	Keith McManus	1985	Jean Menere
	Laurie Clancy	1986	Richard Lunn

VICTORIAN PREMIER'S LITERARY AWARDS

YEAR	AUTHOR	TITLE	CATEGORY
1985	David Malouf	*Antipodes*	Fiction
	Bernard Smith	*The boy Adeodatus*	Non-fiction
	Janet McCalman	*Struggletown*	Australian Studies
	David Allen	*Cheapside*	Drama
	Kevin Hart	*Your shadow*	Poetry
	Rosemary Dobson	*The three fates*	Poetry

1986	Peter Carey	*Illywhacker*	Fiction
	John Bryson	*Evil angels*	Non-fiction
	D. J. Mulvaney and J. H. Calaby	*So much that is new: Baldwin Spencer 1860–1929*	Australian Studies
	Janis Baloois	*Too young for ghosts*	Drama
	Rhyll McMaster	*Washing for money*	Poetry
	John A. Scott	*St Clair*	Poetry

PATRICIA WEICKHARDT AWARD

Awarded annually by the Federation of Australian Writers to an Aboriginal writer.

YEAR	AUTHOR	YEAR	AUTHOR
1976	Dick Roughsey	1981	Bobbi Sykes
1977	Kath Walker	1982	Hyllus Maris
	Linda Walsh	1983	Archie Weller
1978	Kevin Gilbert	1984	James Miller
	Noelene Lane	1985	David Unaipon
1979	Colin Johnson	1986	Bob Merritt
1980	Jack Davis		

PATRICK WHITE AWARD

Awarded annually by a committee to a writer who has been highly creative over a long period but who has not received adequate recognition.

YEAR	AUTHOR	YEAR	AUTHOR
1974	Christina Stead	1980	Bruce Dawe
1975	David Campbell	1981	Dal Stivens
1976	John Blight	1982	Bruce Beaver
1977	Sumner Locke Elliott	1983	Marjorie Barnard
		1984	Rosemary Dobson
1978	Gwen Harwood	1985	Judah Waten
1979	Randolph Stow	1986	John Morrison

ARCHIBALD PRIZE

Awarded annually by the trustees of the Art Gallery of New South Wales for the best portrait submitted by an artist resident in Australia, preferably of a person prominent in art, letters, science or politics.

YEAR	ARTIST	WORK
1921	W. B. McInnes	*Desbrowe Annear*
1922	W. B. McInnes	*Prof Harrison Moore*
1923	W. B. McInnes	*Portrait of a lady*
1924	W. B. McInnes	*Miss Collins*
1925	John Longstaff	*Maurice Moscovitch*
1926	W. B. McInnes	*Silk and lace*
1927	G. W. Lambert	*Mrs Murdoch*
1928	John Longstaff	*Dr Alexander Leeper*
1929	John Longstaff	*W. A. Holman, Esq, KC*
1930	W. B. McInnes	*Drum Major Harry McClelland*
1931	John Longstaff	*Sir John Sulman*

ARCHIBALD PRIZE continued

1932	E. Buckmaster	*Sir William Irvine*
1933	C. Wheeler	*Ambrose Pratt*
1934	H. Hanke	*Self-portrait*
1935	John Longstaff	*A. B. ('Banjo') Paterson*
1936	W. B. McInnes	*Dr Julian Smith*
1937	Normand Baker	*Self-portrait*
1938	Nora Heysen	*Mme Elink Schuurman*
1939	Max Meldrum	*Hon G. C. Bell, Speaker of the House of Representatives*
1940	Max Meldrum	*Dr J. Forbes McKenzie*
1941	W. Dargie	*Sir James Elder, KBE*
1942	W. Dargie	*Corporal Jim Gordon, VC*
1943	William Dobell	*Joshua Smith*
1944	Joshua Smith	*The Hon S. Rosevear, Speaker of the House of Representatives*
1945	W. Dargie	*Lt-General the Hon Edmund Herring, KBE, DSO, MC, ED*
1946	W. Dargie	*L. C. Robson, MC, MA*
1947	W. Dargie	*Sir Marcus Clark, KBE*
1948	William Dobell	*Margaret Olley*
1949	Arthur Murch	*Bonar Dunlop*
1950	W. Dargie	*Sir Leslie McConnan*
1951	Ivor Hele	*Laurie Thomas*
1952	W. Dargie	*Mr Essington Lewis, CH*
1953	Ivor Hele	*Sir Henry Simpson Newland, CBE, DSO, MS, FRCS*
1954	Ivor Hele	*The Rt Hon R. G. Menzies, PC, CH, QC, MP*
1955	Ivor Hele	*Robert Campbell, Esq*
1956	W. Dargie	*Mr Albert Namatjira*
1957	Ivor Hele	*Self-portrait*
1958	W. E. Pidgeon	*Mr Ray Walker*
1959	William Dobell	*Dr Edward McMahon*
1960	Judy Cassab	*Stanislaus Rapotec*
1961	W.E. Pidgeon	*Rabbi Dr I. Porush*
1962	Louis Kahan	*Patrick White*
1963	J. Carrington Smith	*Prof James McAuley*
1964	Not awarded	
1965	Clifton Pugh	*Mr R. A. Henderson*
1966	Jon Molvig	*Charles Blackman*
1967	Judy Cassab	*Margo Lewers*
1968	W. E. Pidgeon	*Lloyd Rees*
1969	Ray Crooke	*George Johnston*
1970	Eric Smith	*Gruzman – architect*
1971	Clifton Pugh	*Sir John McEwen*
1972	Clifton Pugh	*The Hon E. G. Whitlam*
1973	Janet Dawson	*Michael Boddy Reading*
1974	Sam Fullbrook	*Jockey Norman Stephens*
1975	Kevin Connor	*The Hon Sir Frank Kitto, KBE*
1976	Brett Whiteley	*Self-portrait in the studio*
1977	Kevin Connor	*Robert Klippel*
1978	Brett Whiteley	*Art, life and the other thing*
1979	Wes Walters	*Portrait of Philip Adams*
1980	Not awarded	
1981	Eric Smith	*Rudy Komon*
1982	Eric Smith	*Peter Sculthorpe*
1983	Nigel Thomson	*Chandler coventry*
1984	Keith Looby	*Max Gillies*
1985	Guy Warren	*Flugelman with Wingman*
1986	Davida Allen	*Dr John Arthur McKelvey Shera*

H. C. RICHARDS MEMORIAL PRIZE

Held annually 1951–1971. In 1972 replaced by Queensland Art Gallery Trustee Prize, which in 1978 became the Trustees' Purchase Exhibition.

YEAR	ARTIST	WORK
1951	John Rowell	*A northern road*
1952	Charles Bush	*Glasshouse mountains*
1953	Charles Bush	*Near Tumbulgum*
1954	Charles Bush	*Spring Hill, evening*
1955	Arthur Evan Read	*The cane town*
1956	Rhyl Waterhouse	*Old hotel*
1957	Franck de Silva	*Zillmere*
1958	Sali Herman	*Flat-Tops, central Australia*
1959	Max Ragless	*Birdsville*
1960	John Rigby	*Cribb Island*
1961	John Olsen	*Journey into the You Beaut Country no 2*
1962	Margo Lewers	*Bushfire*
1963	Arthur Boyd	*Figure turning into a dragonfly*
1964	Lloyd Rees	*Drama in the valley*
1965	Asher Bilu	*Supernal*
1966	Col Jordon	*Paradox 12*
1967	Sam Fullbrook	*Buderim farmscape*
1968	Michale Smither	*The colander*
1969	Sam Fullbrook	*Portrait study*
1970	Peter Clarke	*Mauve across yellow*
1971	David Aspden	*United 1*

QUEENSLAND ART GALLERY TRUSTEE PRIZE

YEAR	ARTIST	WORK
1972	Sandra Leveson	*Optic series D*
1973	Sydney Ball	*Pawnee summer*
1974	No prize held	
1975	Peter Clarke	*March 30th*
1976	Richard Larter	*Sweet sherry chocolate dip*
1977	Janet Dawson	*Foxy night 2*

TRUSTEES' PURCHASE EXHIBITION

YEAR	ARTIST	WORK
1978	Loueen Morrison	*Reflections in silver* 1977
	David Hugh Schlunke	*Winter* 1978
	Noel Tunks	*Love in idleness* 1976
	James Willebrant	*Evening flight observed* 1979
	Bruce Wilson	*Machine of a dream* 1976
	Rod Withers	*Zoned light industrial* 1977
1979	Henri Bastin	*Gum tree forest* 1978
	Gunter Christmann	*M.S.* 1978
	Shay Docking	*Earth and sea with Barrenjoey* 1978
	Donald Friend	*Pastorale*
	Joy Roggenkamp	*Blown sand* 1979
1980	Robert Boynes	*Red step ladder*
	John Brack	*Procession*
	Jo Davidson	*The garden safe place*
	Angela Gartner	*Cultural cranes*
	J. S. Ostoja-Kotkowski	*Astra*
	Beryl Rojahn	*The Drews' old home, Shorncliffe*

TRUSTEES' PURCHASE EXHIBITION continued

YEAR	ARTIST	WORK
1980	June Stephenson	*Rain cloud over the glass house mountains*
	Michael Winters	*Shirt, shell and summer*
1981	No prize held	
1982	Alfred Engel	*Split planks*
	Mike Nicholas	*Wilderness*
	Michael Shannon	*Abandoned quarry*
	Helen Lillecrap	*Ideas are bound to twig 1*
	Helen Lillecrap	*Ideas are bound to twig 2*
	Jan Senbergs	*Loading*
	John B. Robinson	*Latitudes 1982*

L. J. HARVEY PRIZE FOR DRAWING

Held biennially since 1951.

YEAR	ARTIST	WORK
1951	Kathleen Shillam	*The new-born kid*
1953	Charles Bush	*Rain forest tamborine*
1955	Kathleen Shillam	*Rhinos*
1957	Arthur Evan Read	*Fair-haired girl*
1959	Joy Roggenkamp	*Baby*
1961	Thomas Gleghorn	*Outline of nightfall*
1963	Kenneth Jack	*Murray steamers*
1965	John Aland	*Prospector*
1967	Mervyn Smith	*The dockyard*
1969	Sam Fullbrook	*Slice of melon*
1971	David Rankin	*Untitled*
1973	Nora Heysen	*Dr W. Lister Reid*
1975	Nora Heysen	*Head of a young woman*
1977	Peter Tyndall	*Cocoons art contained within*
1979	Guy Warren	*Balmain drawing no 2*
1981	No prize held	
1983	Jan Senbergs	*Copperopolis–Queenstown*

JOHN MCCAUGHEY MEMORIAL ART PRIZE

Awarded periodically by the National Gallery of Victoria for a painting having as its theme some aspect of the Australian scene and/or way of life.

YEAR	ARTIST	WORK
1957	John Perceval	*Gannets diving*
1958	Noel Counihan	*After work*
1959	Sali Herman	*Country street scene*
1960	Kenneth de Silva	*Come in spinner*
1961	Roger Kemp	*Organized forms*
1965	Gill Jamieson	*The pigs*
1966	Anthony Irving	*Uncle John's 1919 homecoming*
1968	Michael Shannon	*Early morning, Melbourne*
1972	Donald Laycock	*Star cycles*
1975	John Firth-Smith	*From here*
1979	Paul Tartos	*Untitled pink*
	Ken Whisson	*Flag for the City of Sydney*
1981	Imants Tillers	*The modern picture (worlds in collision)*
1983	Craig Gough	*Sandringham series no 18*
	Mandy Martin	*Powerhouse 3*
1987	James Gleeson	*Harbinger*

SULMAN PRIZE

Awarded annually by the trustees of the Art Gallery of New South Wales for the best subject painting, genre painting or design for an intended mural by an artist resident in Australia.

YEAR	ARTIST	YEAR	ARTIST
1936	Henry Hanke	1965	Gareth Jones-Roberts
1937	Not awarded	1966	Louis James
1938	M. C. Meere	1967	Cec Burns
1939	Gert Sellheim	1968	Tim Storrier
1940	Harold Abbott	1969	Louis James
1941	Douglas Annand	1970	Michael Kmit
1942	Jean Bellette	1971	James Meldrum
1943	Elaine Haxton	1972	Peter Powditch
1944	Jean Bellette	1973	Eric Smith
1945	Vergil Lo Schiavo	1974	Keith Looby
1946	Sali Herman	1975	Alan Oldfield and Geoffrey Proud
1947	Douglas Annand	1976	Brett Whiteley
1948	Sali Herman	1977	Salvatore Zofrea
1949	J. Carrington Smith	1978	Brett Whiteley
1950	Harold Greenhill	1979	Salvatore Zofrea
1951	Douglas Annand	1980	Brian Dunlop
1952	Charles Doutney	1981	William Delafield Cook
1953	Eric Smith	1982	Salvatore Zofrea
1954	Wallace Thornton	1983	Nigel Thomson
1955	Wesley Penberthy	1984	Tim Storrier
1956	Harold Greenhill	1985	Victor Morrison Public Art Squad (D. Humphries and R. Monk)
1957	Michael Kmit		
1958	Not awarded		
1959	Susan Wright	1986	Wendy Sharpe
1960	Leonard French		Nigel Thomson
1961	Robin Norling		
1962	John Rigby		
1963	Roy Fluke		
1964	Ken Reinhard		

WYNNE PRIZE

Awarded annually by the trustees of the Art Gallery of New South Wales for a landscape in oils or a sculpture. Since 1961 an additional prize has been offered for a watercolour.

YEAR	ARTIST	YEAR	ARTIST
1897	Walter Withers	1918	W. B. McInnes
1898	W. Lister Lister	1919	Elioth Gruner
1899	G. W. Lambert	1920	Hans Heysen
1900	Walter Withers	1921	Elioth Gruner
1901	W. C. Piguenit	1922	Hans Heysen
1902	James S. White	1923	G. W. L. Hirst
1903	E. Officer	1924	Hans Heysen
1904	Hans Heysen	1925	W. Lister Lister
1905	A. J. Hansen	1926	Hans Heysen
1906	W. Lister Lister	1927	G. Rayner Hoff
1907	G. W. L. Hirst	1928	Arthur Streeton
1908	Will Ashton	1929	Elioth Gruner
1909	Hans Heysen	1930	Will Ashton
1910	W. Lister Lister	1931	Hans Heysen
1911	Hans Heysen	1932	Hans Heysen
1912	W. Lister Lister	1933	Lyndon R. Dadswell
1913	W. Lister Lister	1934	Elioth Gruner
1914	Penleigh Boyd	1935	J. Muir Old
1915	J. C. Wright	1936	Elioth Gruner
1916	Elioth Gruner	1937	Elioth Gruner
1917	W. Lister Lister	1938	Sydney Long

WYNN PRIZE continued

1939	Will Ashton	1968	L. Scott Pendlebury
1940	Sydney Long		Frank McNamara
1941	Lorna Nimmo	1969	John Olsen
1942	Douglas Watson		Frank McNamara
1943	Douglas Dundas	1970	Frederick Bates
1944	Sali Herman		Eva Kubbos
1945	Douglas Watson	1971	Margaret
1946	Lance Solomon		Woodward
1947	Russell Drysdale		Eva Kubbos
1948	William Dobell	1972	Eric Smith
1949	George Lawrence		Kenneth Jack
1950	Lloyd Rees	1973	Clem Millward
1951	Charles Meere		Frank McNamara
1952	Charles Bush	1974	Eric Smith
1953	Lance Solomon		Allan Hondow
1954	Arthur Evan Read	1975	Robert Juniper
1955	Charles Bush		Peter Dorahy
1956	L. Scott Pendlebury	1976	Fred Williams
1957	L. Scott Pendlebury		Fred Williams
1958	Ronald Steuart	1977	Brett Whiteley
1959	Reinis Zusters		Max Miller
1960	John Perceval and L.	1978	Brett Whiteley
	Scott Pendlebury		Fred Williams
1961	David Strachan	1979	Robert Juniper
	Len Annois		Guy Warren
	(watercolour)	1980	William Delafield
1962	Sali Herman		Cook
	Joy Roggenkamp		Elwyn Lynn
1963	Sam Fullbrook	1981	David Voigt
	Eva Kubbos		Eva Kubbos
1964	Sam Fullbrook	1982	Lloyd Rees
	Len Annois		John Wolseley
1965	Sali Herman	1983	David Rankin
	Frederic Bates		Elwyn Lynn
1966	Fred Williams	1984	Brett Whiteley
	Fred Williams		John Caldwell
1967	Sali Herman	1985	John Olsen
	Kenneth Jack	1986	Rosemary Madigan

AUSTRALIAN FILM INSTITUTE AWARD WINNERS

BEST FILM OF THE YEAR
(FORMERLY OPEN GENERAL CATEGORY)

Key	
(GP) = Grand Prix	(S) = Silver
(G) = Gold	(B) = Bronze
	(HM) = Honourable Mention

YEAR	FILM	PRODUCER/CO	DIRECTOR
1958			
1959	Grampians wonderland (S)	D. Swift	Gil Brealey
1960	Anzac (B)	Zanthus Films	Jennie Blackwood
1961	No award		

BEST FILM OF THE YEAR continued

1962	A report on the political development in the territory of Papua New Guinea	Maslyn Williams	S. Benson
1963	A hole in the ground (S)	Aranda Film Productions	Bruce McNaughton
1964	Transfiguration (HM)	Arkaba Film Ltd.	Ludwig Dutigiewicz
1965	Faces in the sun (G)	Cecil Holmes	Cecil Holmes
1966	The Admiral's Cup (B)	Jackson, Wain & Co	Neville Merchant
1967	Interaction: moving and painting (S)	Gil Brealey/ABC	Gil Brealey
1968	The drover's wife (S)	Alan Ashbolt/ABC	Gian Carlo Manara
1969	Jack and Jill: a postscript (S)	Phillip Adams & Brian Robinson	P. Adams & B. Robinson
1970	Three to go: Michael (GP)	Gil Brealey	Peter Weir
1971	Homesdale (G)	Richard Brennan & Grahame Bond	Peter Weir
1972	Stork (G)	Tim Burstall	Tim Burstall
1973	Libido: the child/27A (G)	Tim Burstall/Hadyn Keenan	Tim Burstall/Ebsen Storm
1974/5	Sunday too far away (G)	Gil Brealey & Matt Carroll	Ken Hannam
1976	The Devil's playground	Fred Schepisi	Fred Schepisi
1977	Storm boy	Matt Carroll	Henri Safran
1978	Newsfront	David Elfick	Phil Noyce
1979	My brilliant career	Margaret Fink	Gillian Armstrong
1980	Breaker Morant	Matt Carroll	Bruce Beresford
1981	Gallipoli	Pat Lovell & Robert Stigwood	Peter Weir
1982	Lonely hearts	John B. Murray	Paul Cox
1983	Careful, he might hear you	Jill Robb	Carl Schultz
1984	Annie's coming out	Don Murray	Gil Brealey
1985	Bliss	Anthony Buckley	Ray Lawrence
1986	Malcolm	Nadia Tass & David Parker	Nadia Tass
1987	The year my voice broke	Kennedy Miller	John Duigan

BEST ACHIEVEMENT IN DIRECTION

YEAR	DIRECTOR	FILM
1971	Peter Weir	Homedale
1972	Tim Burstall	Stork
1973	Eric Porter	Marco Polo junior versus the red dragon
1974/5	John Power	Billy and Percy

BEST ACHIEVEMENT IN DIRECTION continued

1976	Fred Schepisi	*The Devil's playground*
1977	Bruce Beresford	*Don's party*
1978	Phil Noyce	*Newsfront*
1979	Gillian Armstrong	*My brilliant career*
1980	Bruce Beresford	*Breaker Morant*
1981	Peter Weir	*Gallipoli*
1982	George Miller	*Mad Max II*
1983	Carl Schultz	*Careful, he might hear you*
1984	Paul Cox	*My first wife*
1985	Ray Lawrence	*Bliss*
1986	Nadia Tass	*Malcolm*
1987	John Duigan	*The year my voice broke*

BEST PERFORMANCE BY AN ACTOR IN A LEADING ROLE

(1958–71 No Award Presented as Part of Presentation)

YEAR	ACTOR	FILM
1972	Bruce Spence	*Stork*
1973	Robert McDarra	*27A*
1974/5	Jack Thompson/ Martin Vaughan	*Petersen & Sunday too far away/Bill and Percy*
1976	Simon Burke and Nick Tate	*The Devil's playground*
1977	John Meillon	*The fourth wish*
1978	Bill Hunter	*Newsfront*
1979	Mel Gibson	*Tim*
1980	Jack Thompson	*Breaker Morant*
1981	Mel Gibson	*Gallipoli*
1982	Ray Barrett	*Goodbye paradise*
1983	Norman Kaye	*Man of flowers*
1984	John Hargreaves	*My first wife*
1985	Chris Haywood	*A street to die*
1986	Colin Friels	*Malcolm*
1987	Leo McKern	*Travelling North*

BEST DOCUMENTARY

YEAR	FILM	DIRECTOR
1958		
1959	*The edge of the deep/ The power makers* (S)	P. Bruce & D. Corke/ L. Robinson
1960	*Three in a million*	Jennie Blackwood
1961	*No award*	
1962	*Bypass to life/Night freighter* (S)	P. Maund/R. Petersen
1963	*The land that waited* (G)	Gil Brealey
1964	*The dancing class/I the Aboriginal* (G)	Tim Cowan/Cecil Holmes
1965	*The legend of Damien Parer/Stronger*	Gil Brealey/Brett Porter
1966	*Concerto for orchestra* (G)	Robert Parker
1967	*Cardin in Australia* (G)	Peter Thompson
1968	*The change at Groote/ The Talgai skull* (G)	Stefan Sargent/Tom Haydon
1969	*Bullocky/The die hard 'The legend of Lasseter's Reef'* (G)	Richard Mitchell/David Crocker
1970	*The gallery* (G)	Philip Mark Law

BEST DOCUMENTARY continued

1971	*A big hand for everyone* (G)	Michael Pearce
1972	*Jackpot town* (G)	Roger Whittaker
1973	*Tidikawa and friends* (G)	J. & S. Doring
1974/5	*Mr symbol man* (G)	Bruce Moir & Bob Kingsbury
1976	*Lalai dreamtime* (B)	Michael Edols
1977	*We are all alone my dears* (S)	Paul Cox
1978	*Growing up series* (S)	Phil Noyce & Jan Sharpe
1979	*Island shunters* (B)	Tim Woolmer
1980	*Frontline*	David Bradbury
1981	*Stepping out*	Chris Noonan
1982	*Angels of war*	Andrew Pike, Hank Nelson & Gavin Dawes
1983	*First contact*	Bob Connolly & Robin Anderson
1984	*Kemira – diary of a strike*	Tom Zubrycki
1985	*Raoul Wallenberg: between the lines*	Bob Weis
1986	*Chile: hasta cuando?*	David Bradbury
1987	*Painting the town*	Trevor Graham & Ned Lander

SUN ARIA WINNERS

YEAR	ARTIST	YEAR	ARTIST
1933	Ruby Zlotowski	1959	Elaine Blight
	Norman Barnes	1960	Roslyn Dunbar
1934	Merle Ambler	1961	Robert Colman
	Robert Nicholson	1962	Valerie Morgan
1935	Phyllis Thompson	1963	Jan Bartlett
	Colin Chapman	1964	Pettine-Ann Croul
1936	Catherine Williams	1965	Serge Baigildin
	Arthur Broadhurst	1966	Patricia Payne
1938	Mildred Walker	1967	Geraldine Hacket-Jones
	Neville Beavis		
1939	Marie Ryan	1968	Bruce Martin
	Raymond Nilsson	1969	Malcolm Donnelly
1940	Nancy Buchanan	1970	Margaret Haggart
	Hugh Godfrey	1971	Richard Greager
1941	Edna McClelland	1972	Carolyn Vaughan
	Allan Ferris	1973	Jonathan Summers
1946	Rosina Raisbeck	1974	Graeme Wall
1947	Eleanor Houston	1975	Carole McKenzie
1948	Florence Taylor	1976	Jenny Lindfield
1949	Joan Sutherland	1977	Rosemary Gunn
1950	June (Gough) Bronhill	1978	Graham MacFarlane
		1979	Joanne Neal
1951	Angelina Arena	1980	Anne Young
1952	Marjorie Conley	1981	Paul Thompson
1953	Tessa Schell	1982	John Antoniou
1954	Jean Brunning	1983	Christine Beasley
1955	Heather Begg	1984	Roger Lemke
1956	Russell Cooper	1985	Michael Howard
1957	Kevin Mills	1986	Deborah Riedel
1958	Heather McMillan		

II
SPORT

CRICKET

AUSTRALIA V ENGLAND

SEASON	VENUE	AUST	ENG	DRAW	AUST CAPTAIN
1876–77	Aust	1	1	–	D. Gregory
1878–79	Aust	1	–	–	D. Gregory
1880	Eng	–	1	–	W. Murdoch
1881–82	Aust	2	–	2	W. Murdoch
1882	Eng	1	–	–	W. Murdoch
1882–83	Aust	2	2	–	W. Murdoch
1884	Eng	–	1	2	W. Murdoch
1884–85	Aust	2	3	–	W. Murdoch (1)
					T. Horan (2)
					H. Massie (1)
					J. Blackham (1)
1886	Eng	–	3	–	H. Scott
1886–87	Aust	–	2	–	P. McDonnell
1887–88	Aust	–	1	–	P. McDonnell
1888	Eng	1	2	–	P. McDonnell
1890	Eng	–	2	–	W. Murdoch
1891–92	Aust	2	1	–	J. Blackham
1893	Eng	–	1	2	J. Blackham
1894–95	Aust	2	3	–	J. Blackham (1)
					G. Giffen (4)
1896	Eng	1	2	–	G. Trott
1897–98	Aust	4	1	–	G. Trott
1899	Eng	1	–	4	J. Darling
1901–02	Aust	4	1	–	J. Darling (3)
					H. Trumble (2)
1902	Eng	2	1	2	J. Darling
1903–04	Aust	2	3	–	M. Noble
1905	Eng	–	2	3	J. Darling
1907–08	Aust	4	1	–	M. Noble
1909	Eng	2	1	2	M. Noble
1911–12	Aust	1	4	–	C. Hill
1912	Eng	–	1	2	S. Gregory
1920–21	Aust	5	–	–	W. Armstrong
1921	Eng	3	–	2	W. Armstrong
1924–25	Aust.	4	1	–	H. Collins
1926	Eng	–	1	4	H. Collins (3)
					W. Bardsley (2)
1928–29	Aust	1	4	–	J. Ryder
1930	Eng	2	1	2	W. Woodfull
1932–33	Aust	1	4	–	W. Woodfull
1934	Eng	2	1	2	W. Woodfull
1936–37	Aust	3	2	–	D. Bradman
1938	Eng	1	1	2	D. Bradman
1946–47	Aust	3	–	2	D. Bradman
1948	Eng	4	–	1	D. Bradman
1950–51	Aust	4	1	–	A. Hassett
1953	Eng	–	1	4	A. Hassett
1954–55	Aust	1	3	1	I. Johnson (4)
					A. Morris (1)
1956	Eng	1	2	2	I. Johnson
1958–59	Aust	4	–	1	R. Benaud
1961	Eng	2	1	2	R. Benaud
1962–63	Aust	1	1	3	R. Benaud
1964	Eng	1	–	4	R. Simpson
1965–66	Aust	1	1	3	R. Simpson (3)
					B. Booth (2)
1968	Eng	1	1	3	W. Lawry (4)
					B. Jarman (1)

AUSTRALIA v ENGLAND continued

SEASON	VENUE	AUST	ENG	DRAW	AUST CAPTAIN
1970–71	Aust	–	2	4	W. Lawry (5)
					I. Chappell (1)
1972	Eng	2	2	1	I. Chappell
1974–75	Aust	4	1	1	I. Chappell
1975	Eng	1	–	3	I. Chappell
1977	Aust	1	–	–	G. Chappell
1977	Eng	–	3	2	G. Chappell
1978–79	Aust	1	5	–	G. Yallop
1979–80	Aust	3	–	–	G. Chappell
1980	Eng	–	–	1	G. Chappell

(This was special Centenary Test played at Lord's.)

SEASON	VENUE	AUST	ENG	DRAW	AUST CAPTAIN
1981	Eng	1	3	2	K. Hughes
1982–83	Aust	2	1	2	G. Chappell
1985	Eng	1	3	2	A. Border
1986–87	Aust	1	2	2	A. Border

AUSTRALIA V INDIA

SEASON	VENUE	AUST	IND	DRAW	AUST CAPTAIN
1947–48	Aust	4	–	1	D. Bradman
1956–57	India	2	–	1	I. Johnson (2)
					R. Lindwall (1)
1959–60	Aust	2	1	2	R. Benaud
1964	India	1	1	1	R. Simpson
1967–68	Aust	4	–	–	R. Simpson (2)
					W. Lawry (2)
1969–70	India	3	1	1	W. Lawry
1977–78	Aust	3	2	–	R. Simpson
1979	India	–	2	4	K. Hughes
1980–81	Aust	1	1	1	G. Chappell
1981	Aust	1	–	2	A. Border
1985–86	Aust	–	–	3	A. Border
1986	India	–	–	2	A. Border

(1 match also tied.)

AUSTRALIA V NEW ZEALAND

SEASON	VENUE	AUST	NZ	DRAW	AUST CAPTAIN
1945–46	NZ	1	–	–	W. Brown
1973–74	Aust	2	–	1	I. Chappell
1974	NZ	1	1	1	I. Chappell
1977	NZ	1	–	1	G. Chappell
1980	Aust	2	–	1	G. Chappell
1982	NZ	1	1	1	G. Chappell
1985	Aust	1	2	–	A. Border
1986	NZ	–	1	2	A. Border

AUSTRALIA V PAKISTAN

SEASON	VENUE	AUST	PAK	DRAW	AUST CAPTAIN
1956–57	Pak	–	1	–	I. Johnson
1959–60	Pak	2	–	1	R. Benaud
1964	Pak	–	–	1	R. Simpson
1964–65	Aust	–	–	1	R. Simpson
1972–73	Aust	3	–	–	I. Chappell
1976–77	Aust	1	1	1	G. Chappell
1979	Aust	1	1	–	G. Yallop
1980	Pak	–	1	2	G. Chappell
1981	Aust	2	1	–	G. Chappell
1982–83	Pak	–	3	–	K. Hughes
1983–84	Aust	2	–	3	K. Hughes

AUSTRALIA V SOUTH AFRICA

SEASON	VENUE	AUST	SA	DRAW	AUST CAPTAIN
1902–03	SA	2	–	1	J. Darling
1910–11	Aust	4	1	–	C. Hill
1912	Eng	2	–	1	S. Gregory
1921–22	SA	1	–	2	H. Collins
1931–32	Aust	5	–	1	W. Woodfull
1935–36	SA	4	–	1	V. Richardson
1949–50	SA	4	–	1	A. Hassett
1952–53	Aust	2	2	1	A. Hassett
1957–58	SA	3	–	2	I. Craig
1963–64	Aust	1	1	3	R. Benaud (1)
					R. Simpson (4)
1966–67	SA	1	3	1	R. Simpson
1970	SA	–	4	–	W. Lawry

AUSTRALIA V SRI LANKA

SEASON	VENUE	AUST	SL	DRAW	AUST CAPTAIN
1983	SL	1	–	–	G. Chappell

(This was the first Test match played between Australia and Sri Lanka.)

AUSTRALIA V WEST INDIES

SEASON	VENUE	AUST	WI	DRAW	AUST CAPTAIN
1930–31	Aust	4	1	–	W. Woodfull
1951–52	Aust	4	1	–	A. Hassett (4)
					A. Morris (1)
1954–55	WI	3	–	2	I. Johnson
1960–61	Aust	2	1	1	R. Benaud

(The First Test of this series, played in Brisbane, resulted in a tie—the first tie in Test cricket. WI scored 453 and 284, Australia 505 and 232.)

SEASON	VENUE	AUST	WI	DRAW	AUST CAPTAIN
1965	WI	1	2	2	R. Simpson
1968–69	Aust	3	1	1	W. Lawry
1973	WI	2	–	3	I. Chappell
1975–76	Aust	5	1	–	G. Chappell
1978	WI	1	3	1	R. Simpson
1979–80	Aust	–	2	1	G. Chappell
1981–82	Aust	1	1	1	G. Chappell
1984	WI	–	3	2	K. Hughes
1984–85	Aust	1	3	1	K. Hughes (2)
					A. Border (3)

SHEFFIELD SHIELD

YEAR	WINNER	YEAR	WINNER
1892–93	Vic	1906–07	NSW
1893–94	SA	1907–08	Vic
1894–95	Vic	1908–09	NSW
1895–96	NSW	1909–10	SA
1896–97	NSW	1910–11	NSW
1897–98	Vic	1911–12	NSW
1898–99	Vic	1912–13	SA
1899–1900	NSW	1913–14	NSW
1900–01	Vic	1914–15	Vic
1901–02	NSW	1915–19	(war years)
1902–03	NSW	1919–20	NSW
1903–04	NSW	1920–21	NSW
1904–05	NSW	1921–22	Vic
1905–06	NSW	1922–23	NSW

SHEFFIELD SHIELD continued

YEAR	WINNER	YEAR	WINNER
1923–24	Vic	1958–59	NSW
1924–25	Vic	1959–60	NSW
1925–26	NSW	1960–61	NSW
1926–27	SA	1961–62	NSW
1927–28	Vic	1962–63	Vic
1928–29	NSW	1963–64	SA
1929–30	Vic	1964–65	NSW
1930–31	Vic	1965–66	NSW
1931–32	NSW	1966–67	Vic
1932–33	NSW	1967–68	WA
1933–34	Vic	1968–69	SA
1934–35	Vic	1969–70	Vic
1935–36	SA	1970–71	SA
1936–37	Vic	1971–72	WA
1937–38	NSW	1972–73	WA
1938–39	SA	1973–74	Vic
1939–40	NSW	1974–75	WA
1940–46	(war years)	1975–76	SA
1946–47	Vic	1976–77	WA
1947–48	WA	1977–78	WA
1948–49	NSW	1978–79	Vic
1949–50	NSW	1979–80	Vic
1950–51	Vic	1980–81	WA
1951–52	NSW	1981–82	SA
1952–53	SA	1982–83	NSW
1953–54	NSW	1983–84	WA
1954–55	NSW	1984–85	NSW
1955–56	NSW	1985–86	NSW
1956–57	NSW	1986–87	WA
1957–58	NSW		

FOOTBALL

RUGBY LEAGUE
(Australian scores listed first)
AUSTRALIA V GREAT BRITAIN

SEASON	VENUE	1st TEST	2nd TEST	3rd TEST
1908–09	Eng	22–22	5–15	5–6
1910	Aust	20–27	13–13	32–15
1911–12	Eng	19–10	11–11	33–8
1914	Aust	5–33	12–7	6–14
1920	Aust	8–4	21–8	13–23
1921–22	Eng	5–6	16–2	0–6
1924	Aust	3–22	3–5	21–11
1928	Aust	12–15	0–8	21–14
1929–30	Eng	31–8	3–9	0–0
		(4th Test won by Eng 3–0)		
1932	Aust	6–8	15–6	13–18
1933	Eng	0–4	5–7	16–19
1936	Aust	24–8	7–12	7–12
1937–38	Eng	4–5	3–13	13–3
1946	Aust	8–8	5–14	7–20
1948–49	Eng	21–23	7–16	9–23
1950	Aust	4–6	15–3	5–2
1952–53	Eng	6–19	5–21	27–7

AUSTRALIA v GREAT BRITAIN continued

1954	Aust	37–12	21–38	20–16
1956–57	Eng	10–21	22–9	0–19
1958	Aust	25–8	18–25	17–40
1959–60	Eng	22–14	10–11	12–18
1962	Aust	12–31	10–17	18–17
1963	Eng	28–2	50–12	5–16
1966	Aust	13–17	6–4	19–14
1967	Eng	11–16	17–11	11–3
1970	Aust	37–15	7–28	17–21
1973	Eng	11–21	14–6	15–5
1974	Aust	12–6	11–16	22–18
1978	Eng	15–9	14–18	23–6
1979	Aust	35–0	24–16	28–2
1982	Eng	40–3	27–6	32–8
1984	Aust	25–8	18–6	20–7
1986	Eng	38–16	34–4	24–15

AUSTRALIA V FRANCE
(Australian scores listed first)

SEASON	VENUE	1st TEST	2nd TEST	3rd TEST
1937–38	France	35–6	16–11	—
1948–49	France	29–10	10–0	—
1951	Aust	15–26	23–11	14–35
1952–53	France	16–12	0–5	5–13
1955	Aust	20–8	28–29	5–8
1956–57	France	15–8	10–6	25–21
1959–60	France	20–19	17–2	16–8
1960	Aust	8–8	56–6	5–7
1963–64	France	5–8	21–9	16–8
1964	Aust	20–6	27–2	35–9
1967	France	7–7	3–10	13–16
1973	France	21–9	14–3	—
1978	France	10–13	10–11	—
1981	Aust	43–3	17–2	—
1982	France	15–4	23–9	—
1986	France	44–2	52–0	—

AUSTRALIA V NEW ZEALAND
(Australian scores listed first)

SEASON	VENUE	1st TEST	2nd TEST	3rd TEST
1908	Aust	12–24	14–9	—
1909	Aust	11–19	10–5	25–5
1919	NZ	44–21	10–26	34–23
		(4th Test won by Aust 32–2)		
1935	NZ	14–22	29–8	31–8
1937	NZ	12–8	13–15	—
1948	Aust	19–21	13–4	—
1949	NZ	21–16	13–10	—
1952	Aust	25–13	25–49	9–19
1953	NZ	5–25	11–12	18–16
1956	Aust	12–9	8–2	31–14
1959	Aust	9–8	38–10	12–28
1961	NZ	10–12	10–8	—
1963	Aust	7–3	13–16	14–0
1965	NZ	13–8	5–7	—
1967	Aust	22–13	35–22	13–9
1969	NZ	20–10	14–18	—
1971	NZ	24–3	—	—
1972	Aust	36–11	31–7	—
1978	Aust	24–2	38–7	33–16

AUSTRALIA v NEW ZEALAND continued

1980	NZ	27–6	15–6	—
1982	Aust	11–8	20–2	—
1983	NZ/Aust	16–4	12–19	—
1985	Aust/NZ	26–20	10–6	0–18
1986	NZ/Aust	22–8	29–12	32–12

SYDNEY FIRST GRADE RUGBY LEAGUE PREMIERSHIP

YEAR	WINNER	YEAR	WINNER
1908	South Sydney	1948	Western Suburbs
1909	South Sydney	1949	St George
1910	Newtown	1950	South Sydney
1911	Eastern Suburbs	1951	South Sydney
1912	Eastern Suburbs	1952	Western Suburbs
1913	Eastern Suburbs	1953	South Sydney
1914	South Sydney	1954	South Sydney
1915	Balmain	1955	South Sydney
1916	Balmain	1956	St George
1917	Balmain	1957	St George
1918	South Sydney	1958	St George
1919	Balmain	1959	St George
1920	Balmain	1960	St George
1921	North Sydney	1961	St George
1922	North Sydney	1962	St George
1923	Eastern Suburbs	1963	St George
1924	Balmain	1964	St George
1925	South Sydney	1965	St George
1926	South Sydney	1966	St George
1927	South Sydney	1967	South Sydney
1928	South Sydney	1968	South Sydney
1929	South Sydney	1969	Balmain
1930	Western Suburbs	1970	South Sydney
1931	South Sydney	1971	South Sydney
1932	South Sydney	1972	Manly-Warringah
1933	Newtown	1973	Manly-Warringah
1934	Western Suburbs	1974	Eastern Suburbs
1935	Eastern Suburbs	1975	Eastern Suburbs
1936	Eastern Suburbs	1976	Manly-Warringah
1937	Eastern Suburbs	1977	St George
1938	Canterbury-Bankstown	1978	Manly-Warringah
1939	Balmain	1979	St George
1940	Eastern Suburbs	1980	Canterbury-Bankstown
1941	St George	1981	Parramatta
1942	Canterbury-Bankstown	1982	Parramatta
1943	Newtown	1983	Parramatta
1944	Balmain	1984	Canterbury-Bankstown
1945	Eastern Suburbs	1985	Canterbury-Bankstown
1946	Balmain	1986	Parramatta
1947	Balmain	1987	Manly-Warringah

BRISBANE FIRST GRADE RUGBY LEAGUE PREMIERSHIP

YEAR	WINNER	YEAR	WINNER
1909	Valley	1916	Western Suburbs
1910	Ipswich	1917	Valley
1911	Valley-Toombul	1918	Valley
1912	Natives	1919	Valley
1913	West End	1920	Western Suburbs
1914	Valley	1921	Carlton
1915	Valley	1922	Western Suburbs

BRISBANE FIRST GRADE continued

1923	Coorparoo	1956	Brothers
1924	Valley	1957	Valley
1925	Carlton	1958	Brothers
1926	Brothers	1959	Northern Suburbs
1927	Grammar	1960	Northern Suburbs
1928	University	1961	Northern Suburbs
1929	University	1962	Northern Suburbs
1930	Carlton	1963	Northern Suburbs
1931	Valley	1964	Northern Suburbs
1932	Western Suburbs	1965	Redcliffe
1933	Valley	1966	Northern Suburbs
1934	Northern Suburbs	1967	Brothers
1935	Brothers	1968	Brothers
1936	Western Suburbs	1969	Northern Suburbs
1937	Valley	1970	Valley
1938	Northern Suburbs	1971	Valley
1939	Brothers	1972	Eastern Suburbs
1940	Northern Suburbs	1973	Valley
1941	Valley	1974	Valley
1942	Brothers	1975	Western Suburbs
1943	Brothers	1976	Western Suburbs
1944	Valley	1977	Eastern Suburbs
1945	Southern Suburbs	1978	Eastern Suburbs
1946	Valley	1979	Valley
1947	Eastern Suburbs	1980	Northern Suburbs
1948	Western Suburbs	1981	Southern Suburbs
1949	Southern Suburbs	1982	Wynnum Manly
1950	Eastern Suburbs	1983	Eastern Suburbs
1951	Southern Suburbs	1984	Wynnum Manly
1952	Western Suburbs	1985	Southern Suburbs
1953	Southern Suburbs	1986	Wynnum Manly
1954	Western Suburbs	1987	Brothers
1955	Valley		

RUGBY UNION
(Australian scores listed first)
AUSTRALIA V BRITISH ISLES

SEASON	1st TEST	2nd TEST	3rd TEST
1899	13–3	0–11	10–11
	(British Isles won 4th Test 13–0)		
1904	0–17	3–17	0–16
1930	6–5	—	—
1950	6–19	3–24	—
1959	6–17	3–24	—
1966	8–11	0–31	—

AUSTRALIA V ENGLAND

SEASON	1st TEST	2nd TEST	3rd TEST
1909	9–3	—	—
1948	11–0	—	—
1958	6–9	—	—
1963	18–9	—	—
1967	23–11	—	—
1973	3–20	—	—
1975	16–9	30–21	—
1975–76	6–23	—	—
1982	11–15	—	—
1984	19–3	—	—
1987	19–6	—	—

AUSTRALIA V NEW ZEALAND

SEASON	1st TEST	2nd TEST	3rd TEST
1903	3–22	—	—
1905	3–14	—	—
1907	6–26	5–14	5–5
1910	0–6	11–0	13–28
1913	5–30	13–25	16–5
1914	0–5	0–17	7–22
1929	9–8	17–9	15–13
1931	13–20	—	—
1932	22–17	3–21	13–21
1934	25–11	3–3	—
1936	6–11	13–38	—
1938	9–24	14–20	6–14
1946	8–31	10–14	—
1947	5–13	14–27	—
1949	11–6	16–9	—
1951	0–8	11–17	6–16
1952	14–9	8–15	—
1955	0–8	8–16	8–3
1957	11–25	9–22	—
1958	3–25	6–3	8–17
1962	6–20	5–14	9–9
1962	0–3	8–16	—
1964	9–14	3–18	20–5
1967	9–29	—	—
1968	11–27	18–19	—
1972	6–29	17–30	3–38
1974	6–11	16–16	6–16
1978	12–13	6–22	30–16
1979	12–6	—	—
1980	13–9	9–12	26–10
1982	16–23	19–16	18–33
1983	8–18	—	—
1984	16–9	15–19	24–25
1985	9–10	—	—
1986	13–12	12–13	22–9

AUSTRALIA V SOUTH AFRICA

SEASON	1st TEST	2nd TEST	3rd TEST
1933	3–17	21–6	3–12
	(4th Test: 0–11; 5th Test: 15–4)		
1937	5–9	17–21	—
1953	3–25	18–14	8–18
	(4th Test: 9–22)		
1956	0–9	0–9	—
1961	3–28	11–23	—
1963	3–14	9–5	11–9
	(4th Test: 6–22)		
1965	18–11	12–8	—
1969	11–30	9–16	3–11
	(4th Test: 8–19)		
1971	11–19	6–14	6–18

AUSTRALIA V SCOTLAND

SEASON	1st TEST	2nd TEST	3rd TEST
1947	16–7	—	—
1958	8–12	—	—
1966	5–11	—	—
1968	3–9	—	—
1970	23–3	—	—

AUSTRALIA v SCOTLAND continued

1975–76	10–36	—	—
1982	7–12	33–9	—
1984	37–12	—	—

AUSTRALIA V IRELAND

SEASON	1st TEST	2nd TEST	3rd TEST
1947	16–3	—	—
1958	6–9	—	—
1967	8–15	5–11	—
1968	3–10	—	—
1975–76	26–10	—	—
1979	12–27	3–9	—
1981	16–12	—	—
1984	16–9	—	—

AUSTRALIA V WALES

SEASON	1st TEST	2nd TEST	3rd TEST
1908	6–9	—	—
1947	0–6	—	—
1958	3–9	—	—
1966	14–11	—	—
1969	16–19	—	—
1973	0–24	—	—
1975–76	3–28	—	—
1978	18–8	19–17	—
1981	13–18	—	—
1984	28–9	—	—

AUSTRALIA V FRANCE

SEASON	1st TEST	2nd TEST	3rd TEST
1948	6–13	—	—
1958	0–19	—	—
1961	8–15	—	—
1967	14–20	—	—
1968	11–10	—	—
1971	13–11	9–18	—
1972	14–14	15–16	—
1976	15–18	16–34	—
1981	17–15	24–14	—
1983	15–15	6–15	—
1986	27–14	—	—

AUSTRALIA V FIJI

SEASON	1st TEST	2nd TEST	3rd TEST
1952	15–9	15–17	—
1954	22–19	16–18	—
1961	24–6	20–14	3–3
1972	21–19	—	—
1976	22–6	21–9	27–17
1980	22–9	—	—
1984	16–3	—	—
1985	52–28	31–9	—

BRISBANE FIRST GRADE
RUGBY UNION PREMIERSHIP

YEAR	WINNER	YEAR	WINNER
1887	Ipswich Rangers	1951	Christian Brothers
1888	Union Harriers	1952	University
1889	Wallaroos	1953	Christian Brothers

BRISBANE FIRST GRADE continued

YEAR	WINNER	YEAR	WINNER
1890	Wallaroos	1954	University
1891	Arfoma	1955	University
1892	Past & Present Grammar	1956	University
1893	Boomerangs	1957	University
1894	Boomerangs	1958	Southern Districts
1895	City	1959	Christian Brothers
1896	City	1960	University
1897	City	1961	GPS Old Boys
1898	Past Grammar	1962	University
1899	Past Grammar	1963	Teachers
1900	City	1964	University
1901	North Brisbane	1965	University
1902	North Brisbane	1966	Brothers
1903	North Brisbane	1967	University
1904	North Brisbane and Valley	1968	Brothers
1905–14	No records kept	1969	University
1915	Brothers	1970	University
1929	YMCA	1971	Brothers
1930	University	1972	GPS Old Boys
1931	University	1973	Brothers
1932	University	1974	Brothers
1933	YMCA	1975	Brothers
1934	University	1976	Teachers-Norths
1935	Eagle Junction	1977	Western Suburbs
1936	Eagle Junction	1978	Brothers
1937	Eagle Junction	1979	University
1938	Eagle Junction	1980	Brothers
1939	YMCA	1981	Brothers
1940–45	No competition	1982	Brothers
1946	Christian Brothers Old Boys	1983	Brothers
1947	University	1984	Brothers
1948	University	1985	Wests
1949	Christian Brothers	1986	Souths
1950	Christian Brothers	1987	Brothers

SYDNEY FIRST GRADE
RUGBY UNION PREMIERSHIP

YEAR	WINNER	YEAR	WINNER
1900	Glebe	1921	Eastern Suburbs
1901	Glebe and University	1922	Manly
1902	Western Suburbs	1923	University
1903	Eastern Suburbs	1924	University
1904	University	1925	Glebe and Balmain
1905	South Sydney	1926	University
1906	Glebe	1927	University
1907	Glebe	1928	University
1908	Newtown	1929	Western Suburbs
1909	Glebe	1930	Randwick
1910	Newtown	1931	Eastern Suburbs
1911	Newtown	1932	Manly
1912	Glebe	1933	Northern Suburbs
1913	Eastern Suburbs	1934	Randwick
1914	Glebe	1935	Northern Suburbs
1915–18	No Competition	1936	Drummoyne
1919	University	1937	University
1920	University	1938	Randwick
1939	University	1964	Northern Suburbs
1940	Randwick	1965	Randwick
1941	Eastern Suburbs	1966	Randwick

SYDNEY FIRST GRADE continued

Year	Winner	Year	Winner
1942	Manly	1967	Randwick
1943	Manly	1968	University
1944	Eastern Suburbs	1969	Eastern Suburbs
1945	University	1970	University
1946	Eastern Suburbs	1971	Randwick
1947	Eastern Suburbs	1972	University
1948	Randwick	1973	Randwick
1949	Gordon	1974	Randwick
1950	Manly	1975	Northern Suburbs
1951	University	1976	Gordon
1952	Gordon	1977	Parramatta
1953	University	1978	Randwick
1954	University	1979	Randwick
1955	University	1980	Randwick
1956	Gordon	1981	Randwick
1957	St George	1982	Randwick
1958	Gordon	1983	Manly
1959	Randwick	1984	Randwick
1960	Northern Suburbs	1985	Parramatta
1961	University	1986	Parramatta
1962	University	1987	Randwick
1963	Northern Suburbs		

Australian Rules
Victorian Football League (VFL) Premiers

YEAR	WINNER	YEAR	WINNER
1897	Essendon	1927	Collingwood
1898	Fitzroy	1928	Collingwood
1899	Fitzroy	1929	Collingwood
1900	Melbourne	1930	Collingwood
1901	Essendon	1931	Geelong
1902	Collingwood	1932	Richmond
1903	Collingwood	1933	S Melbourne
1904	Fitzroy	1934	Richmond
1905	Fitzroy	1935	Collingwood
1906	Carlton	1936	Collingwood
1907	Carlton	1937	Geelong
1908	Carlton	1938	Carlton
1909	S Melbourne	1939	Melbourne
1910	Collingwood	1940	Melbourne
1911	Essendon	1941	Melbourne
1912	Essendon	1942	Essendon
1913	Fitzroy	1943	Richmond
1914	Carlton	1944	Fitzroy
1915	Carlton	1945	Carlton
1916	Fitzroy	1946	Essendon
1917	Collingwood	1947	Carlton
1918	S Melbourne	1948	Melbourne
1919	Collingwood	1949	Essendon
1920	Richmond	1950	Essendon
1921	Richmond	1951	Geelong
1922	Fitzroy	1952	Geelong
1923	Essendon	1953	Collingwood
1924	Essendon	1954	Footscray
1925	Geelong	1955	Melbourne
1926	Melbourne	1956	Melbourne

VFL PREMIERS continued

Year	Winner	Year	Winner
1957	Melbourne	1973	Richmond
1958	Collingwood	1974	Richmond
1959	Melbourne	1975	N Melbourne
1960	Melbourne	1976	Hawthorn
1961	Hawthorn	1977	N Melbourne
1962	Essendon	1978	Hawthorn
1963	Geelong	1979	Carlton
1964	Melbourne	1980	Richmond
1965	Essendon	1981	Carlton
1966	St Kilda	1982	Carlton
1967	Richmond	1983	Hawthorn
1968	Carlton	1984	Essendon
1969	Richmond	1985	Essendon
1970	Carlton	1986	Hawthorn
1971	Hawthorn	1987	Carlton
1972	Carlton		

South Australian Premiers

YEAR	WINNER	YEAR	WINNER
1878	Norwood	1921	Pt Adelaide
1879	Norwood	1922	Norwood
1880	Norwood	1923	Norwood
1881	Norwood	1924	W Torrens
1882	Norwood	1925	Norwood
1883	Norwood	1926	Sturt
1884	Pt Adelaide	1927	W Adelaide
1885	S Adelaide	1928	Pt Adelaide
1886	Adelaide	1929	Norwood
1887	Norwood	1930	N Adelaide
1888	Norwood	1931	N Adelaide
1889	Norwood	1932	Sturt
1890	Pt Adelaide	1933	W Torrens
1891	Norwood	1934	Glenelg
1892	S Adelaide	1935	S Adelaide
1893	S Adelaide	1936	Pt Adelaide
1894	Norwood	1937	Pt Adelaide
1895	S Adelaide	1938	S Adelaide
1896	S Adelaide	1939	Pt Adelaide
1897	Pt Adelaide	1940	Sturt
1898	S Adelaide	1941	Norwood
1899	S Adelaide	1942–44	No competition
1900	N Adelaide	1945	W Torrens
1901	Norwood	1946	Norwood
1902	N Adelaide	1947	W Adelaide
1903	Pt Adelaide	1948	Norwood
1904	Norwood	1949	N Adelaide
1905	N Adelaide	1950	Norwood
1906	Pt Adelaide	1951	Pt Adelaide
1907	Norwood	1952	N Adelaide
1908	W Adelaide	1953	W Torrens
1909	W Adelaide	1954	Pt Adelaide
1910	Pt Adelaide	1955	Pt Adelaide
1911	W Adelaide	1956	Pt Adelaide
1912	W Adelaide	1957	Pt Adelaide
1913	Pt Adelaide	1958	Pt Adelaide
1914	Pt Adelaide	1959	Pt Adelaide
1915	Sturt	1960	N Adelaide
1916–18	No competition	1961	W Adelaide
1919	Sturt	1962	Pt Adelaide
1920	N Adelaide	1963	Pt Adelaide

SOUTH AUSTRALIAN PREMIERS continued

1964	S Adelaide	1976	Sturt
1965	Pt Adelaide	1977	Pt Adelaide
1966	Sturt	1978	Norwood
1967	Sturt	1979	Pt Adelaide
1968	Pt Adelaide	1980	Pt Adelaide
1969	Sturt	1981	Pt Adelaide
1970	Sturt	1982	Norwood
1971	N Adelaide	1983	W Adelaide
1972	N Adelaide	1984	Norwood
1973	N Adelaide	1985	Glenelg
1974	Sturt	1986	Glenelg
1975	Norwood	1987	N Adelaide

TASMANIAN AUSTRALIAN NATIONAL FOOTBALL LEAGUE (TFL) PREMIERS

YEAR	WINNER	YEAR	WINNER
1945	N Hobart	1967	N Hobart
1946	Sandy Bay	1968	New Norfolk
1947	N Hobart	1969	N Hobart
1948	New Town	1970	Clarence
1949	New Town	1971	Sandy Bay
1950	Hobart	1972	Sandy Bay
1951	New Town	1973	Hobart
1952	Sandy Bay	1974	N Hobart
1953	New Town	1975	Glenorchy
1954	Hobart	1976	Sandy Bay
1955	New Town	1977	Sandy Bay
1956	New Town	1978	Sandy Bay
1957	N Hobart	1979	Clarence
1958	Glenorchy	1980	Hobart
1959	Hobart	1981	Clarence
1960	Hobart	1982	New Norfolk
1961	N Hobart	1983	Glenorchy
1962	N Hobart	1984	Glenorchy
1963	Hobart	1985	Glenorchy
1964	Sandy Bay	1986	Glenorchy
1965	Glenorchy	1987	N Hobart
1966	Hobart		

WESTERN AUSTRALIAN PREMIERS

YEAR	WINNER	YEAR	WINNER
1885	Fremantle	1904	E Fremantle
1886	Unions	1905	W Perth
1887	Fremantle	1906	E Fremantle
1888	Fremantle	1907	Perth
1889	Fremantle	1908	E Fremantle
1890	Fremantle	1909	E Fremantle
1891	Fremantle	1910	E Fremantle
1892	Fremantle	1911	E Fremantle
1893	Fremantle	1912	Subiaco
1894	Fremantle	1913	Subiaco
1895	Fremantle	1914	E Fremantle
1896	Fremantle	1915	Subiaco
1897	W Perth	1916	S Fremantle
1898	Fremantle	1918	E Fremantle
1899	W Perth	1919	E Perth
1900	E Fremantle	1920	E Perth
1901	W Perth	1921	E Perth
1902	E Fremantle	1922	E Perth
1903	E Fremantle	1923	E Perth

WESTERN AUSTRALIAN PREMIERS continued

1924	Subiaco	1956	E Perth
1925	E Fremantle	1957	E Perth
1926	E Perth	1958	E Fremantle
1927	E Perth	1959	E Perth
1928	E Fremantle	1960	W Perth
1929	E Fremantle	1961	Swan District
1930	E Fremantle	1962	Swan District
1931	E Fremantle	1963	Swan District
1932	W Perth	1964	Claremont
1933	E Fremantle	1965	E Fremantle
1934	W Perth	1966	Perth
1935	W Perth	1967	Perth
1936	E Perth	1968	Perth
1937	E Fremantle	1969	W Perth
1938	Claremont	1970	S Fremantle
1939	Claremont	1971	W Perth
1940	Claremont	1972	E Perth
1941	W Perth	1973	Subiaco
1942	W Perth	1974	E Fremantle
1943	E Fremantle	1975	W Perth
1944	E Perth	1976	Perth
1945	E Fremantle	1977	Perth
1946	E Fremantle	1978	E Perth
1947	S Fremantle	1979	E Fremantle
1948	S Fremantle	1980	S Fremantle
1949	W Perth	1981	Claremont
1950	S Fremantle	1982	Swan District
1951	W Perth	1983	Swan District
1952	S Fremantle	1984	Swan District
1953	S Fremantle	1985	Fremantle
1954	E Fremantle	1986	Subiaco
1955	S Fremantle	1987	Claremont

MELBOURNE CUP RESULTS 1861–1984

YEAR	WINNER	JOCKEY	S/P	FIELD
1861	Archer	J. Cutts	6/1	17
1862	Archer	J. Cutts	2/1	20
1863	Banker	H. Chifney	10/1	7
1864	Lantern	S. Davis	15/1	19
1865	Tory Boy	E. Cavanagh	20/1	23
1866	The Barb	W. Davis	6/1	28
1867	Tim Whiffler	I. Driscoll	5/2	27
1868	Glencoe	C. Stanley	10/1	25
1869	Warrior	J. Morrison	10/1	26
1870	Nimblefoot	J. Day	12/1	28
1871	The Pearl	J. Cavanagh	100/1	23
1872	The Quack	W. Enderson	5/1	22
1873	Don Juan	W. Wilson	3/1	24
1874	Haricot	P. Piggot	15/1	18
1875	Wollomai	R. Batty	16/1	20
1876	Briseis	P. St Albans	7/1	33
1877	Chester	P. Piggot	5/1	33
1878	Calamia	T. Brown	10/1	30
1879	Darriwell	S. Cracknell	33/1	27
1880	Grand Flaneur	T. Hales	4/1	22
1881	Zulu	J. Gough	33/1	33
1882	The Assyrian	C. Hutchins	33/1	25

MELBOURNE CUP continued

1883	Martini Henri	J. Williamson	3/1	29
1884	Malua	A. Robertson	6/1	24
1885	Sheet Anchor	M. O'Brien	14/1	35
1886	Arsenal	W. English	20/1	28
1887	Dunlop	T. Sanders	20/1	18
1888	Mentor	M. O'Brien	7/1	28
1889	Bravo	J. Anwin	8/1	20
1890	Carbine	R. Ramage	4/1	39
1891	Malvolio	G. Redfern	14/1	34
1892	Glenloth	G. Robson	50/1	35
1893	Tarcoola	H. Cripps	40/1	30
1894	Patron	H. G. Dawes	33/1	28
1895	Auraria	J. Stevenson	33/1	36
1896	Newhaven	H. Gardiner	4/1	25
1897	Gaulus	S. Callinan	14/1	29
1898	The Grafter	J. Gough	8/1	28
1899	Meriwee	V. Turner	7/1	28
1900	Clean Sweep	R. Richardson	20/1	29
1901	Revenue	F. Dunn	7/4	19
1902	The Victory	R. Lewis	25/1	22
1903	Lord Cardigan	N. Godby	5/1	24
1904	Acrasia	T. Clayton	14/1	34
1905	Blue Spec	F. Bullock	10/1	27
1906	Poseidon	T. Clayton	4/1	21
1907	Apologue	W. Evans	3/1	19
1908	Lord Nolan	J. R. Flynn	16/1	22
1909	Prince Foote	W. H. McLachlan	4/1	26
1910	Comedy King	W. H. McLachlan	10/1	30
1911	The Parisian	R. Cameron	5/1	33
1912	Piastre	A. Shanahan	7/1	23
1913	Posinatus	A. Shanahan	15/1	20
1914	Kingsburgh	G. Meddick	20/1	28
1915	Patrobus	R. Lewis	8/1	24
1916	Sasanof	F. Foley	12/1	28
1917	Westcourt	W. H. McLachlan	4/1	20
1918	Nighwatch	W. Duncan	12/1	27
1919	Artilleryman	R. Lewis	10/1	20
1920	Poitrel	K. Bracken	8/1	23
1921	Sister Olive	E. O'Sullivan	16/1	25
1922	King Ingoda	A. Wilson	8/1	32
1923	Bitalli	A. Wilson	4/1	26
1924	Backwood	P. Brown	8/1	18
1925	Windbag	J. Munro	5/1	28
1926	Spearfelt	H. Cairns	10/1	21
1927	Trivalve	R. Lewis	6/1	26
1928	Statesman	J. Munro	7/2	17
1929	Nightmarch	R. Reed	6/1	14
1930	Phar Lap	J. E. Pike	8/11	15
1931	White Nose	N. Percival	8/1	14
1932	Peter Pan	W. Duncan	4/1	27
1933	Hall Mark	J. O'Sullivan	4/1	18
1934	Peter Pan	D. Munro	14/1	22
1935	Marabou	K. Voitre	9/2	22
1936	Wotan	O. Philips	100/1	20
1937	The Trump	A. Reed	11/2	28
1938	Catalogue	F. Shean	25/1	22
1939	Rivette	E. Preston	5/1	26
1940	Old Rowley	A. Knox	100/1	20
1941	Skipton	W. Cook	8/1	23
1942	Colonus	H. McCloud	33/1	24
1943	Dark Felt	V. Hartney	7/2	24

MELBOURNE CUP continued

1944	Sirius	D. Munro	3/1	23
1945	Rainbird	W. Cook	12/1	26
1946	Russia	D. Munro	16/1	35
1947	Hiraji	J. Purtell	12/1	30
1948	Rimfire	R. Neville	80/1	30
1949	Foxzami	W. Fellows	16/1	31
1950	Comic Court	P. Glennon	25/1	26
1951	Delta	N. Sellwood	10/1	28
1952	Dalray	W. Williamson	5/1	30
1953	Wodalla	J. Purtell	14/1	21
1954	Rising Fast	J. Purtell	5/2	25
1955	Toparoa	N. Sellwood	6/1	24
1956	Evening Peal	G. Podmore	15/1	22
1957	Straight Draw	N. McGrowdie	13/1	19
1958	Baystone	M. Schumacher	10/1	29
1959	Macdougal	P. Glennon	8/1	28
1960	Hi Jinx	W. A. Smith	50/1	32
1961	Lord Fury	R. Selkrig	20/1	25
1962	Even Stevens	L. Coles	3/1	26
1963	Gatum Gatum	J. Johnson	25/1	26
1964	Polo Prince	R. Taylor	12/1	26
1965	Light Fingers	R. Higgins	15/1	26
1966	Galilee	J. Miller	11/2	22
1967	Red Handed	R. Higgins	4/1	22
1968	Rain Lover	J. Johnson	7/1	26
1969	Rain Lover	J. Johnson	8/1	23
1970	Baghdad Note	E. Didman	25/1	23
1971	Silver Knight	R. Marsh	10/1	21
1972	Piping Lane	J. Letts	40/1	22
1973	Gala Supreme	F. Reys	9/1	24
1974	Think Big	H. White	12/1	22
1975	Think Big	H. White	33/1	21
1976	Van Der Hum	R. Skelton	9/2	23
1977	Gold & Black	J. Duggan	7/2	24
1978	Arwon	H. White	5/1	22
1979	Hyperno	H. White	7/1	22
1980	Beldale Ball	J. Letts	11/1	22
1981	Just A Dash	P. Cook	15/1	22
1982	Gurner's Lane	L. Dittman	8/1	23
1983	Kiwi	J. A. Cassidy	9/1	24
1984	Black Knight	P. Cook	10/1	19
1985	What A Nuisance	P. Hyland	15/1	23
1986	At Talaq	M. Clarke	10/1	22
1987	Kensei	L. Olsen	12/1	21

TENNIS
DAVIS CUP

YEAR	WINNER	VERSUS		SCORE
1900	United States	v	British Isles	3–0
1901	No challenge			
1902	United States	v	British Isles	3–2
1903	British Isles	v	United States	4–1
1904	British Isles	v	Belgium	5–0
1905	British Isles	v	United States	5–0
1906	British Isles	v	United States	5–0
1907	Australasia	v	British Isles	3–2

DAVIS CUP continued

1908	Australasia	v	United States	3–2
1909	Australasia	v	United States	5–0
1910	No challenge			
1911	Australasia	v	United States	5–0
1912	British Isles	v	Australasia	3–2
1913	United States	v	British Isles	3–2
1914	Australasia	v	United States	3–2
1915–18	No challenge			
1919	Australasia	v	British Isles	4–1
1920	United States	v	Australasia	5–0
1921	United States	v	Japan	5–0
1922	United States	v	Australasia	4–1
1923	United States	v	Australia	4–1
1924	United States	v	Australia	5–0
1925	United States	v	France	5–0
1926	United States	v	France	4–1
1927	France	v	United States	3–2
1928	France	v	United States	4–1
1929	France	v	United States	3–2
1930	France	v	United States	4–1
1931	France	v	Great Britain	3–2
1932	France	v	United States	3–2
1933	Great Britain	v	France	3–2
1934	Great Britain	v	United States	4–1
1935	Great Britain	v	United States	5–0
1936	Great Britain	v	Australia	3–2
1937	United States	v	Great Britain	4–1
1938	United States	v	Australia	3–2
1939	Australia	v	United States	3–2
1940–45	No challenge			
1946	United States	v	Australia	5–0
1947	United States	v	Australia	4–1
1948	United States	v	Australia	5–0
1949	United States	v	Australia	4–1
1950	Australia	v	United States	4–1
1951	Australia	v	United States	3–2
1952	Australia	v	United States	4–1
1953	Australia	v	United States	3–2
1954	United States	v	Australia	3–2
1955	Australia	v	United States	5–0
1956	Australia	v	United States	5–0
1957	Australia	v	United States	3–2
1958	United States	v	Australia	3–2
1959	Australia	v	United States	3–2
1960	Australia	v	Italy	4–1
1961	Australia	v	Italy	5–0
1962	Australia	v	Mexico	5–0
1963	United States	v	Australia	3–2
1964	Australia	v	United States	3–2
1965	Australia	v	Spain	4–1

DAVIS CUP continued

1966	Australia	v	India	4–1
1967	Australia	v	Spain	4–1
1968	United States	v	Australia	4–1
1969	United States	v	Romania	5–0
1970	United States	v	West Germany	5–0
1971	United States	v	Romania	3–2
1972	United States	v	Romania	3–2
1973	Australia	v	United States	5–0
1974	South Africa	v	India (by default)	
1975	Sweden	v	Czechoslovakia	3–2
1976	Italy	v	Chile	4–1
1977	Australia	v	Italy	3–1
1978	United States	v	Great Britain	4–1
1979	United States	v	Italy	5–0
1980	Czechoslovakia	v	Italy	4–1
1981	United States	v	Argentina	3–1
1982	United States	v	France	4–1
1983	Australia	v	Sweden	3–2
1984	Sweden	v	United States	4–1
1985	Sweden	v	West Germany	3–2
1986	Australia	v	Sweden	3–2

FEDERATION CUP

YEAR		DEFEATED	
1963	United States	d	Australia
1964	Australia	d	United States
1965	Australia	d	United States
1966	United States	d	West Germany
1967	United States	d	Great Britain
1968	Australia	d	Netherlands
1969	United States	d	Australia
1970	Australia	d	West Germany
1971	Australia	d	Great Britain
1972	South Africa	d	Great Britain
1973	Australia	d	South Africa
1974	Australia	d	United States
1975	Czechoslovakia	d	Australia
1976	United States	d	Australia
1977	United States	d	Australia
1978	United States	d	Australia
1979	United States	d	Australia
1980	United States	d	Australia
1981	United States	d	Great Britain
1982	United States	d	West Germany
1983	Czechoslovakia	d	West Germany
1984	Czechoslovakia	d	Australia
1985	Czechoslovakia	d	United States
1986	United States	d	Czechoslovakia
1987	West Germany	d	United States

III
GOVERNMENT

GOVERNORS-GENERAL OF THE COMMONWEALTH OF AUSTRALIA

Administrators appointed between Governor-Generalships are included.

1 Jan 1901–
9 Jan 1903
Earl of Hopetoun (John Adrian Louis Hope), PC, KT, GCMG, GCVO, Governor-General and Commander-in-Chief of the Commonwealth of Australia.

17 July 1902–
9 Jan 1903
Lord Tennyson (Hallam Tennyson), Governor-General (Acting).

9 Jan 1903–
21 Jan 1904
Lord Tennyson (Hallam Tennyson), GCMG, Governor-General.

21 Jan 1904–
9 Sept 1908
Lord Northcote (Henry Stafford Northcote), PC, GCMG, GCIE, CB, Governor-General.

9 Sept 1908–
31 July 1911
Earl of Dudley (William Humble Ward), PC, GCMG, GCVO, Governor-General.

31 July 1911–
18 May 1914
Lord Denman (Thomas Denman), PC, GCMG, GCVO, Governor-General.

18 May 1914–
6 Oct 1920
The Rt Hon Sir Ronald Craufurd Munro-Ferguson, GCMG, Governor-General.

6 Oct 1920–
8 Oct 1925
Lord Forster (Henry William Forster), PC, GCMG, Governor-General.

8 Oct 1925–
2 Oct 1930
Lord Stonehaven (Sir John Lawrence Baird), PC, GCMG, DSO, Governor-General.

3 Oct 1930–
22 Jan 1931
Lord Somers (Arthur Herbert Tennyson Somers Cocks), KCMG, DSO, MC, officer administering the Government of the Commonwealth of Australia.

22 Jan 1931–
22 Jan 1936
The Rt Hon Sir Isaac Alfred Isaacs, GCMG, Governor-General.

23 Jan 1936–
30 Jan 1945
Lord Gowrie (Brigadier-General Alexander Gore Arkwright Hore-Ruthven), VC, PC, GCMG, CB, DSO, Governor-General.

5 Sept 1944–
30 Jan 1945
Major-General Sir Winston Dugan, GCMG, CB, DSO, officer administering the Government of the Commonwealth of Australia.

30 Jan 1945–
11 May 1947
His Royal Highness Prince Henry William Frederick Albert, Duke of Gloucester, Earl of Ulster and Baron Culloden, KG, PC, KT, KP, GCB, GCMG, GCVO, Governor-General.

19 Jan 1947–
11 Mar 1947
Major-General Sir Winston Dugan, GCMG, CB, DSO, officer administering the Government of the Commonwealth of Australia.

11 Mar 1947–
8 May 1953
Sir William John McKell, GCMG, Governor-General.

8 May 1953–
2 Feb 1960
Field Marshal Sir William Joseph Slim, KG, GCB, GCMG, GCVO, GBE, DSO, MC, Governor-General.

2 Feb 1960–
3 Feb 1961
Viscount Dunrossil (William Shepherd Morrison), PC, GCMG, MC, KStJ, Governor-General.

GOVERNORS-GENERAL continued

4 Feb 1961–
3 Aug 1961
General Sir Reginald Alexander Dallas Brooks, KCB, KCMG, KCVO, DSO, KStJ, officer administering the Government of the Commonwealth of Australia.

3 Aug 1961–
22 Sept 1965
Viscount De L'Isle (William Philip Sidney), VC, PC, GCMG, GCVO, KStJ, Governor-General.

7 May 1965–
22 Sept 1965
Colonel Sir Henry Abel Smith, KCMG, KCVO, DSO, KStJ, officer administering the Government of the Commonwealth of Australia.

22 Sept 1965–
30 Apr 1969
Lord Casey (Richard Gardiner Casey), KG, PC, GCMG, CH, DSO, MC, KStJ, Governor-General.

30 Apr 1969–
11 July 1974
The Rt Hon Sir Paul Meernaa Caedwalla Hasluck, GCMG, GCVO, KStJ, Governor-General.

11 July 1974–
8 Dec 1977
The Rt Hon Sir John Robert Kerr, AK, GCMG, GCVO, KStJ, Governor-General.

8 Dec 1977–
20 July 1982
The Rt Hon Sir Zelman Cowen, AK, GCMG, KStJ, QC, Governor-General.

20 July 1982–
The Rt Hon Sir Ninian Martin Stephen, PC, KBE, Governor-General.

GOVERNORS OF NEW SOUTH WALES

26 Jan 1788–
10 Dec 1792
Captain Arthur Phillip, RN, Captain-General and Governor-in-Chief in and over the Territory called New South Wales and its Dependencies.

11 Dec 1792–
12 Dec 1794
Major Francis Grouse administered the settlement.

12 Dec 1794–
11 Sept 1795
Captain William Patterson administered the settlement.

11 Sept 1795–
27 Sept 1800
Captain John Hunter, RN, Governor.

28 Sept 1800–
12 Aug 1806
Captain Philip Gidley King, RN, Governor.

13 Aug 1806–
26 Jan 1808
Captain William Bligh, RN, Governor.

26 Jan 1808–
28 July 1808
Major George Johnston administered the colony.

29 July 1808–
8 Jan 1809
Lieutenant-Colonel Joseph Foveaux administered the colony.

9 Jan 1809–
31 Dec 1809
Colonel William Paterson administered the colony.

1 Jan 1810–
1 Dec 1821
Major-General Lachlan Macquarie, Governor.

1 Dec 1821–
1 Dec 1825
Major-General Sir Thomas Makdougall Brisbane, KCB, Governor.

1 Dec 1825–
18 Dec 1825
Lieutenant-Colonel William Stewart administered the colony.

19 Dec 1825–
21 Oct 1831
Lieutenant-General Ralph Darling, Governor.

22 Oct 1831– 2 Dec 1831	Colonel Patrick Lindesay administered the colony.
3 Dec 1831– 3 Dec 1837	Major-General Sir Richard Bourke, KCB, Governor.
6 Dec 1837– 23 Feb 1838	Lieutenant-Colonel Kenneth Snodgrass administered the colony.
24 Feb 1838– 11 July 1846	Sir George Gipps, Governor.
12 July 1846– 2 Aug 1846	Sir Maurice Charles Philip O'Connell, KCH, administered the colony.
3 Aug 1846– 1 Jan 1851	Sir Charles Augustus Fitz Roy, KCH, Governor.
2 Jan 1851– 17 Jan 1855	Sir Charles Augustus Fitz Roy, KCB, KCH, Captain-General of New South Wales, Victoria, Van Diemen's Land and South Australia and Governor-General of the said colonies and Western Australia.
20 Jan 1855– 19 Dec 1855	Sir William Thomas Denison, KCB, Governor-General of Her Majesty's Colonies of New South Wales, Tasmania, Victoria, South Australia and Western Australia.
19 Dec 1855– 22 Jan 1861	Sir William Thomas Denison, KCB, Captain-General and Governor-in-Chief of New South Wales and its Dependencies and Vice-Admiral of the same [additional commission].
22 Jan 1861– 22 Mar 1861	Lieutenant-Colonel John Francis Kempt administered the colony.
22 Mar 1861– 24 Dec 1867	The Rt Hon Sir John Young, Bt, GCMG, KCB, Captain-General, Governor-in-Chief and Vice-Admiral of New South Wales and its Dependencies.
25 Dec 1867– 7 Jan 1868	Major-General Sir Trevor Chute, KCB, administered the colony.
8 Jan 1868– 22 Feb 1872	Earl of Belmore (Sir Somerset Richard Lowry-Corry), PC Ireland, GCMG, Governor and Commander-in-Chief of the Colony of New South Wales and Vice-Admiral of the same.
23 Feb 1872– 2 June 1872	Sir Alfred Stephen, CB, administered the colony.
3 June 1872– 19 Mar 1879	Sir Hercules George Robert Robinson, GCMG, Governor.
20 Mar 1879– 3 Aug 1879	Sir Alfred Stephen, KCMG, CB, administered the colony.
4 Aug 1879– 9 Nov 1885	Lord Augustus William Frederick Spencer Loftus, PC, GCB, Governor and Commander-in-Chief of New South Wales and its Dependencies.
10 Nov 1885– 11 Dec 1885	Sir Alfred Stephen, GCMG, CB, administered the colony.
12 Dec 1885– 3 Nov 1890	Lord Carrington (Charles Robert Wynn-Carrington), PC, GCMG, Governor.

3 Nov 1890– 15 Jan 1891	Sir Alfred Stephen, GCMG, CB, administered the colony.
15 Jan 1891– 2 Mar 1893	Earl of Jersey (Victor Albert George Child Villiers), PC, GCMG, Governor.
3 Mar 1893– 29 May 1893	Sir Frederick Darley administered the colony.
29 May 1893– 15 Mar 1895	The Rt Hon Sir Robert William Duff, GCMG, Governor.
16 Mar 1895– 22 Nov 1895	Sir Frederick Darley administered the colony.
22 Nov 1895– 5 Mar 1899	Viscount Hampden (Henry Robert Brand), GCMG, Governor.
5 Mar 1899– 18 May 1899	Sir Frederick Darley, KCMG, administered the colony.
18 May 1899– 31 Dec 1900	Earl Beauchamp (William Lygon), KCMG, Governor.
1 Jan 1901– 30 Apr 1901	Earl Beauchamp (William Lygon), KCMG, Governor in and over the State of New South Wales and its Dependencies.
1 Nov 1900– 27 May 1902	Sir Frederick Darley, GCMG, administered the state in the absence of Lord Beauchamp.
27 May 1902– 24 Mar 1909	Admiral Sir Harry Holdsworth Rawson, KCB, Governor.
24 Mar 1909– 27 May 1909	Sir George Bowen Simpson, the Acting Chief Justice, administered the state.
28 May 1909– 11 Mar 1913	Lord Chelmsford (Frederic John Napier Thesiger), GCMG, Governor.
11 Mar 1913– 14 Mar 1913	Sir William Cullen, KCMG, administered the state.
14 Mar 1913– 27 Oct 1917	Sir Gerald Strickland, KCMG, Governor.
28 Oct 1917– 17 Feb 1918	Sir William Cullen, KCMG, administered the state.
18 Feb 1918– 16 Sept 1923	Sir Walter Edward Davidson, KCMG, Governor.
16 Sept 1923– 27 Feb 1924	Sir William Cullen, KCMG, administered the state.
28 Feb 1924– 8 Apr 1930	Admiral Sir Dudley Rawson Stratford De Chair, KCB, MVO, Governor.
9 Apr 1930– 28 May 1930	Sir William Cullen, KCMG, administered the state.
29 May 1930– 15 Jan 1935	Air Vice-Marshal Sir Philip Woolcott Game, GBE, KCB, DSO, Governor.
15 Jan 1935– 20 Feb 1935	Sir Philip Whistler Street administered the state.
21 Feb 1935– 22 Jan 1936	Brigadier-General the Honourable Sir Alexander Gore Arkwright Hore-Ruthven, VC, GCMG, CB, DSO, Governor.
22 Jan 1936– 6 Aug 1936	Sir Philip Whistler Street, KCMG, administered the state.
6 Aug 1936– 29 Oct 1936	Admiral Sir David Murray Anderson, KCB, KCMG, MVO, Governor.

GOVERNORS OF NEW SOUTH WALES continued

29 Oct 1936–
8 Apr 1937
Sir Philip Whistler Street, KCMG, administered the state.

8 Apr 1937–
6 June 1945
Lord Wakehurst (The Honourable John de Vere Loder), KCMG, Governor.

6 June 1945–
1 Aug 1946
Sir Frederick Jordan, KCMG, administered the state.

1 Aug 1946–
31 July 1957
General Sir John Northcott, KCMG, KCVO, CB, Governor.

1 Aug 1957–
31 July 1965
Lieutenant-General Sir Eric Winslow Woodward, KCMG, KCVO, CB, CBE, DSO, Governor.

3 Aug 1965–
20 Jan 1966
Sir Kenneth Whistler Street administered the state.

20 Jan 1966–
20 Jan 1981
Sir Arthur Roden Cutler, VC, KCMG, KCVO, CBE, KStJ, Governor.

20 Jan 1981–
Air Marshal Sir James Rowland, KBE, DFC, AFC, KStJ, BE (Aero), FRAeS, C Eng, Governor.

GOVERNORS OF VICTORIA

30 Sept 1839–
15 July 1851
Charles Joseph La Trobe, Superintendent of the District of Port Phillip.

15 July 1851–
5 May 1854
Charles Joseph La Trobe, Lieutenant-Governor of the colony of Victoria.

6 May 1854–
22 June 1854
John Vesey Fitzgerald administered the colony.

22 June 1854–
21 May 1855
Captain Sir Charles Hotham, RN, KCB, Lieutenant-Governor.

22 May 1855–
31 Dec 1855
Captain Sir Charles Hotham, RN, KCB, Captain-General and Governor-in-Chief of the Colony of Victoria, also Vice-Admiral, Commissary, and Deputy in the office of Vice-Admiralty in the said colony.

1 Jan 1856–
26 Dec 1856
Major-General Edward Macarthur administered the colony.

26 Dec 1856–
10 Sept 1863
Sir Henry Barkly, KCB, Captain-General and Governor-in-Chief of the Colony of Victoria, and Vice-Admiral of the same.

11 Sept 1863–
7 May 1866
Sir Charles Henry Darling, KCB, Governor and Commander-in-Chief.

7 May 1866–
15 Aug 1866
Brigadier-General George Jackson Carey administered the colony.

15 Aug 1866–
2 Mar 1873
Sir John Henry Thomas Manners-Sutton, KCB, Governor and Commander-in-Chief.

3 Mar 1873–
30 July 1873
Sir George Ferguson Bowen administered the colony.

30 July 1873–
22 Feb 1879
Sir George Ferguson Bowen, GCMG, Governor and Commander-in-Chief of the Colony of Victoria and its Dependencies, and Vice-Admiral of the same.

GOVERNORS OF VICTORIA continued

27 Feb 1879–
29 Apr 1879
Marquess of Normanby administered the colony.

29 Apr 1879–
18 Apr 1884
Marquess of Normanby (George Augustus Constantine Phipps), PC, GCMG, Governor and Commander-in-Chief.

18 Apr 1884–
15 July 1884
Sir William Foster Stawell administered the colony.

15 July 1884–
15 Nov 1889
Sir Henry Brougham Loch, GCMG, KCB, Governor and Commander-in-Chief.

16 Nov 1889–
27 Nov 1889
Sir William Cleaver Francis Robinson administered the colony.

28 Nov 1889–
12 July 1895
Earl of Hopetoun (John Adrian Louis Hope), GCMG, Governor and Commander-in-Chief.

27 Mar 1895–
24 Oct 1895
Sir John Madden administered the colony.

25 Oct 1895–
31 Mar 1900
Lord Brassey (Thomas Brassey), KCB, Governor and Commander-in-Chief.

15 Jan 1900–
2 Jan 1901
Sir John Madden administered the Colony of Victoria.

2 Jan 1901–
10 Dec 1901
Sir John Madden administered the State of Victoria.

10 Dec 1901–
24 Nov 1903
Sir George Sydenham Clarke, KCMG, Governor of the State of Victoria.

24 Nov 1903–
25 Apr 1904
Sir John Madden administered the state.

25 Apr 1904–
6 July 1908
Major-General Sir Reginald Arthur James Talbot, KCB, Governor.

6 July 1908–
26 July 1908
Sir John Madden administered the state.

27 July 1908–
19 May 1911
Sir Thomas David Gibson Carmichael, Bt, KCMG, Governor.

19 May 1911–
24 May 1911
Sir John Madden administered the state.

24 May 1911–
31 Jan 1914
Sir John Michael Fleetwood Fuller, Bt, KCMG, Governor.

28 Aug 1913–
23 Feb 1914
Sir John Madden administered the state.

23 Feb 1914–
30 Jan 1920
Sir Arthur Lyulph Stanley, KCMG, Governor.

31 Jan 1920–
24 Feb 1921
Sir William Hill Irvine administered the state.

24 Feb 1921–
7 Apr 1926
Earl of Stradbroke (Colonel George Edward John Mowbray Rous), KCMG, CB, CVO, CBE, Governor.

8 Apr 1926–
27 June 1926
Sir William Hill Irvine administered the state.

28 June 1926–
23 June 1931
Lord Somers (Lieutenant-Colonel Arthur Herbert Tennyson Somers Cocks), KCMG, MC, Governor.

24 June 1931–
13 May 1934
Sir William Hill Irvine administered the state.

14 May 1934–
4 Apr 1939
Lord Huntingfield (Captain William Charles Arcedeckne Vanneck), KCMG, Governor.

5 Apr 1939–
16 July 1939
Sir Frederick Wollaston Mann administered the state.

17 July 1939–
20 Feb 1949
Major-General Sir Winston Joseph Dugan, GCMB, CB, DSO, Governor.

21 Feb 1949–
17 Oct 1949
Lieutenant-General Sir Edmund Francis Herring administered the state.

18 Oct 1949–
7 July 1953
General Sir Reginald Alexander Dallas Brooks, KCB, CMG, DSO, Governor.

8 July 1953–
23 Nov 1953
Sir Charles Lowe administered the state.

24 Nov 1953–
7 May 1963
General Sir Reginald Alexander Dallas Brooks, KCB, KCMG, KCVO, DSO, Governor.

8 May 1963–
31 May 1974
Major-General Sir Rohan Delacombe, KCMG, KCVO, KBE, CB, DSO, Governor.

24 May 1974–
2 June 1974
Sir Henry Winneke administered the state.

3 June 1974–
1 Mar 1982
Sir Henry Winneke, KCMG, KCVO, OBE, KStJ, QC, Governor.

1 Mar 1982–
3 Oct 1985
Rear-Admiral Sir Brian Murray, KCMG, AO, KStJ, Governor.

4 Oct 1985–
17 Feb 1986
Sir John Young, KCMG, AO, Lieutenant-Governor and Chief Justice administered the state.

18 Feb 1986–
Rev Dr John Davis McCaughey, Governor.

GOVERNORS OF QUEENSLAND

10 Dec 1859–
4 Jan 1868
Sir George Ferguson Bowen, GCMG, Captain-General and Governor-in-Chief of the Colony of Queensland and its Dependencies, and Vice-Admiral.

4 Jan 1868–
14 Aug 1868
Sir Maurice Charles O'Connell administered the colony.

14 Aug 1868–
2 Jan 1871
Colonel Samuel Wensley Blackall, Governor and Commander-in-Chief of the colony and its Dependencies.

2 Jan 1871–
12 Aug 1871
Sir Maurice Charles O'Connell administered the colony.

12 Aug 1871–
12 Nov 1874
Marquess of Normanby (George Augustus Constantine Phipps), PC, Governor.

12 Nov 1874–
23 Jan 1875
Sir Maurice Charles O'Connell administered the colony.

23 Jan 1875–
14 Mar 1877
William Wellington Cairns, CMG, Governor.

14 Mar 1877–
10 Apr 1877
Sir Maurice Charles O'Connell administered the colony.

11 Apr 1877–
20 July 1877
Sir Arthur Edward Kennedy administered the colony.

20 July 1877–
2 May 1883
Sir Arthur Edward Kennedy, GCMG, CB, Governor.

2 May 1883–
6 Nov 1883
Sir Arthur Hunter Palmer administered the colony.

6 Nov 1883–
9 Oct 1888
Sir Anthony Musgrave, KCMG, Governor.

9 Oct 1888–
1 May 1889
Sir Arthur Hunter Palmer administered the colony.

1 May 1889–
31 Dec 1895
General Sir Henry Wylie Norman, GCB, GCMG, CIE, Governor.

15 Nov 1895–
9 Apr 1896
Sir Arthur Hunter Palmer administered the colony.

9 Apr 1896–
31 Dec 1900
Lord Lamington (Charles Wallace Alexander Napier Cochrane Baillie), KCMG, Governor.

1 Jan 1901–
19 Dec 1901
Lord Lamington (Charles Wallace Alexander Napier Cochrane Baillie), KCMG, Governor in and over the State of Queensland and its Dependencies.

21 June 1901–
24 Mar 1902
Sir Samuel Griffith administered the state.

24 Mar 1902–
10 Oct 1904
Major-General Sir Herbert Charles Chermside, GCMG, CB, Governor.

10 Oct 1904–
30 Nov 1905
Sir Hugh Muir Nelson administered the state.

20 Nov 1905–
26 May 1909
Lord Chelmsford (Frederic John Napier Thesiger), KCMG, Governor.

27 May 1909–
2 Dec 1909
Sir Arthur Morgan administered the state.

2 Dec 1909–
16 July 1914
Sir William Macgregor, GCMG, CB, Governor.

16 July 1914–
15 Mar 1915
Sir Arthur Morgan administered the state.

15 Mar 1915–
3 Feb 1920
Major Sir Hamilton John Goold-Adams, GCMG, CG, Governor.

3 Feb 1920–
3 Dec 1920
William Lennon administered the state.

3 Dec 1920–
27 Oct 1925
The Rt Hon Lieutenant-Colonel Sir Matthew Nathan, GCMG, Governor.

27 Oct 1925–
13 June 1927
William Lennon administered the state.

13 June 1927–
7 Apr 1932
Lieutenant-General Sir Thomas Herbert John Chapman Goodwin, KCB, CMG, DSO, Governor.

8 Apr 1932–
1 June 1932
Sir James William Blair, Chief Justice, administered the state.

13 June 1932–
16 May 1937
Colonel Sir Leslie Orme Wilson, GCSI, GCIE, CMG, DSO, Governor.

17 May 1937–
21 Nov 1937
Sir James William Blair administered the state.

22 Nov 1937–
23 Apr 1946
Colonel Sir Leslie Orme Wilson, GCSI, GCMG, GCIE, DSO, Governor.

GOVERNORS OF QUEENSLAND continued

24 Apr 1946–
30 Sept 1946
Frank Arthur Cooper administered the state.

1 Oct 1946–
4 Dec 1957
Lieutenant-General Sir John Dudley Lavarack, KCVO, KBE, CB, CMG, DSO, Governor.

4 Dec 1957–
18 Mar 1958
Sir Alan Mansfield administered the state.

18 Mar 1958–
20 Mar 1966
Colonel Sir Henry Abel Smith, KCMG, KCVO, Governor.

21 Mar 1966–
20 Mar 1972
Sir Alan Mansfield, KCMG, KCVO, Governor.

21 Mar 1972–
20 Mar 1977
Air Marshal Sir Colin Hannah, KCMG, KBE, CB, Governor.

21 Mar 1977–
21 Apr 1977
Sir Mostyn Hanger, KBE, Chief Justice, administered the state.

22 Apr 1977–
21 July 1985
Commodore Sir James Maxwell Ramsay, KCMG, KCVO, CBE, DSC, KStJ, Governor.

22 July 1985–
Sir Walter Benjamin Campbell, QC, Governor.

GOVERNORS OF SOUTH AUSTRALIA

28 Dec 1836–
16 July 1838
Captain John Hindmarsh, RN, KH, Governor and Commander-in-Chief of the Province of South Australia.

16 July 1838–
17 Oct 1838
George Milner Stephen administered the colony.

17 Oct 1838–
15 May 1841
Lieutenant-Colonel George Gawler, KH, Resident Commissioner.

15 May 1841–
25 Oct 1845
Captain George Grey, Governor and Commander-in-Chief of the Province of South Australia.

25 Oct 1845–
2 Aug 1848
Lieutenant-Colonel Frederick Holt Robe, Lieutenant-Governor.

2 Aug 1848–
20 Dec 1854
Sir Henry Edward Fox Young, Lieutenant-Governor.

20 Dec 1854–
8 June 1855
Boyle Travers Finniss administered the colony.

8 June 1855–
4 Mar 1862
Sir Richard Graves MacDonnell, CB, Captain-General and Governor-in-Chief of the Province of South Australia and Vice-Admiral of the same.

4 Mar 1862–
19 Feb 1868
Sir Dominick Daly, Governor.

20 Feb 1868–
15 Feb 1869
Lieutenant-Colonel Francis Gilbert Hamley administered the colony.

16 Feb 1869–
18 Apr 1873
The Rt Hon Sir James Fergusson, Bt, Governor and Commander-in-Chief in and over the Colony of South Australia and its Dependencies.

7 Dec 1872–
8 June 1873
Sir Richard Davies Hanson administered the colony.

GOVERNORS OF SOUTH AUSTRALIA continued

9 June 1873–
29 Jan 1877
Sir Anthony Musgrave, KCMG, Governor.

29 Jan 1877–
24 Mar 1877
Chief Justice S. J. Way administered the colony.

24 Mar 1877–
17 May 1877
Sir W. W. Cairns administered the colony.

17 May 1877–
2 Oct 1877
Chief Justice S. J. Way administered the colony.

2 Oct 1877–
9 Jan 1883
Sir William Francis Drummond Jervois, GCMG, CB, Governor.

9 Jan 1883–
19 Feb 1883
Chief Justice S. J. Way administered the colony.

19 Feb 1883–
5 Mar 1889
Sir William Cleaver Francis Robinson, GCMG, Governor.

6 Mar 1889–
11 Apr 1889
Chief Justice S. J. Way administered the colony.

11 Apr 1889–
10 Apr 1895
Earl of Kintore (Algernon Hawkins Thomond Keith-Falconer), PC, GCMG, Governor.

17 Jan 1895–
29 Oct 1895
Chief Justice S. J. Way administered the colony.

29 Oct 1895–
29 Mar 1899
Sir Thomas Fowell Buxton, Bt, GCMG, Governor.

30 Sept 1898–
10 Apr 1899
Chief Justice S. J. Way administered the colony.

10 Apr 1899–
31 Dec 1900
Lord Tennyson (Hallam Tennyson), KCMG, Governor.

1 Jan 1901–
17 July 1902
Lord Tennyson (Hallam Tennyson), KCMG, Governor in and over the State of South Australia and its Dependencies.

17 July 1902–
1 July 1903
Sir Samuel Way administered the state.

1 July 1903–
18 Feb 1909
Sir George Ruthven Le Hunte, KCMG, Governor.

2 Jan 1909–
29 Mar 1909
Sir Samuel Way administered the state.

29 Mar 1909–
22 Mar 1914
Admiral Sir Day Hort Bosanquet, GCVO, KCB, Governor.

2 Feb 1914–
18 Apr 1914
Sir Samuel Way administered the state.

18 Apr 1914–
30 Apr 1920
Lieutenant-Colonel Sir Henry Lionel Galway, KCMG, DSO, Governor.

10 Feb 1920–
9 June 1920
Sir George Murray administered the state.

9 June 1920–
30 May 1922
Lieutenant-Colonel Sir William Ernest George Archibald Weigall, KCMG, Governor.

24 Apr 1922–
4 Dec 1922
Sir George Murray administered the state.

4 Dec 1922–
4 Dec 1927
Lieutenant-General Sir George Tom Molesworth Bridges, KCB, KCMG, DSO, Governor.

6 Dec 1927– 13 May 1928	Sir George Murray administered the state.
14 May 1928– 26 Apr 1934	Brigadier-General Sir Alexander Gore Arkwright Hore-Ruthven, VC, KCMG, CB, DSO, Governor.
27 Apr 1934– 27 July 1934	Sir George Murray administered the state.
28 July 1934– 23 Feb 1939	Major-General Sir Winston Joseph Dugan, KCMG, CB, DSO, Governor.
24 Feb 1939– 11 Aug 1939	Sir George Murray administered the state.
12 Aug 1939– 26 Apr 1944	Sir Charles Malcolm Barclay-Harvey, KCMG, Governor.
19 Dec 1944– 18 June 1952	Lieutenant-General Sir Charles Willoughby Moke Norrie, KCMG, CB, DSO, MC, Governor.
23 Feb 1953– 7 Mar 1960	Air Vice-Marshal Sir Robert Allingham George, KCVO, KBE, CB, MC, Governor.
5 Apr 1961– 1 June 1968	Lieutenant-General Sir Edric Montague Bastyan, KCMG, KBE, CB, Governor.
1 June 1968– 4 Dec 1968	Sir John Mellis Napier administered the state.
4 Dec 1968– 15 Sept 1971	Major-General Sir James William Harrison, KCMG, CB, CBE, Governor.
15 Sept 1971– 1 Dec 1971	Sir John Mellis Napier administered the state.
1 Dec 1971– 30 Nov 1976	Sir Mark (Marcus Laurence Elwin) Oliphant, AC, KBE, KStJ, Governor.
1 Dec 1976– 30 Apr 1977	Sir Douglas (Ralph) Nicholls, KCVO, OBE, KStJ, Governor.
30 Apr 1977– 1 Sept 1977	Walter R. Crocker, KBE, administered the state.
1 Sept 1977– 28 Mar 1982	Sir Keith Douglas Seaman, KCVO, OBE, KStJ, Governor.
23 Apr 1982–	Lieutenant-General Sir Donald Dunstan, KBE, GB, KStJ, Governor.

GOVERNORS OF WESTERN AUSTRALIA

30 Dec 1828– 5 Feb 1832	Captain James Stirling, RN, Lieutenant-Governor, Commander-in-Chief, and Vice-Admiral of the Colony of Western Australia.
6 Feb 1832– 11 Aug 1832	Captain James Stirling, RN, Governor, Commander-in-Chief, and Vice-Admiral of the Colony of Western Australia.
12 Aug 1832– 13 Sept 1833	Captain Frederick Chidley Irwin administered the colony.
14 Sept 1833– 10 May 1834	Captain Richard Daniell administered the colony.
11 May 1834– 23 May 1834	Captain Picton Beete administered the colony.

24 May 1834– 18 Aug 1834	Captain Richard Daniell administered the colony.
19 Aug 1834– 2 Jan 1839	Captain Sir James Stirling, RN, Governor.
3 Jan 1839– 26 Jan 1846	John Hutt, Governor.
27 Jan 1846– 11 Feb 1847	Lieutenant-Colonel Andrew Clarke, KH, Governor.
12 Feb 1847– 11 Aug 1848	Lieutenant-Colonel Frederick Chidley Irwin, Governor.
12 Aug 1848– 22 July 1855	Captain Charles Fitzgerald, RN, Governor.
23 July 1855– 19 Feb 1862	Arthur Edward Kennedy, Governor.
20 Feb 1862– 27 Feb 1862	Brevet Lieutenant-Colonel John Bruce administered the colony.
28 Feb 1862– 1 Nov 1868	John Stephen Hampton, Governor.
2 Nov 1868– 29 Sept 1869	Lieutenant-Colonel John Bruce administered the colony.
30 Sept 1869– 3 Jan 1875	Frederick Aloysius Weld, Governor and Commander-in-Chief of Western Australia and its Dependencies.
4 Jan 1875– 10 Jan 1875	Lieutenant-Colonel E. D. Harvest administered the colony.
11 Jan 1875– 6 Sept 1877	William Cleaver Francis Robinson, CMG, Governor.
7 Sept 1877– 11 Nov 1877	Lieutenant-Colonel E. D. Harvest administered the colony.
12 Nov 1877– 29 Jan 1878	Major-General Sir Harry St George Ord, KCMG, CB, Lieutenant-Governor.
30 Jan 1878– 9 Apr 1880	Major-General Sir Harry St George Ord, KCMG, CB, Governor.
10 Apr 1880– 13 Feb 1883	Sir William Cleaver Francis Robinson, KCMG, Governor.
14 Feb 1883– 1 June 1883	Henry (later Sir Henry) Thomas Wrenfordsley administered the colony.
2 June 1883– 20 Dec 1889	Sir Frederick Napier Broome, KCMG, Governor.
21 Dec 1889– 19 Oct 1890	Sir Malcolm Fraser administered the colony.
20 Oct 1890– 17 Mar 1895	Sir William Cleaver Francis Robinson, GCMG, Governor.
18 Mar 1895– 22 Dec 1895	Sir Alexander Campbell Onslow administered the colony.
23 Dec 1895– 29 June 1900	Lieutenant-Colonel Sir Gerard Smith, KCMG, Governor.
30 June 1900– 3 Mar 1901	Sir Alexander Campbell Onslow administered the colony.
4 Mar 1901– 30 Apr 1901	Edward Albert Stone administered the state.

GOVERNORS OF WESTERN AUSTRALIA continued

1 May 1901– 13 Aug 1902	Captain Sir Arthur Lawley, KCMG, Governor of the State of Western Australia and its Dependencies.
14 Aug 1902– 23 Mar 1903	Sir Edward Stone administered the state.
24 Mar 1903– 22 Apr 1909	Admiral Sir Frederick George Denham Bedford, GCB, Governor.
23 Apr 1909– 30 May 1909	Sir Edward Stone administered the state.
31 May 1909– 3 Mar 1913	Sir Gerald Strickland, KCMG, Governor.
4 Mar 1913– 16 Mar 1913	Sir Edward Stone administered the state.
17 Mar 1913– 26 Feb 1917	Major-General Sir Harry Barron, KCMG, CVO, Governor.
27 Feb 1917– 8 Apr 1917	Sir Edward Stone, KCMG, administered the state.
9 Apr 1917– 8 Apr 1920	The Rt Hon Sir William Grey Ellison-Macartney, KCMG, Governor.
9 Apr 1920– 16 June 1924	Sir Francis Alexander Newdigate Newdegate, KCMG, Governor.
17 June 1924– 27 Oct 1924	Sir Robert Furs McMillan administered the state.
28 Oct 1924– 8 June 1931	Colonel Sir William Robert Campion, KCMG, DSO, Governor.
9 June 1931– 29 June 1932	Sir John Alfred Northmore, KCMG, administered the state.
30 June 1932– 10 July 1933	Sir John Alfred Northmore, KCMG, Lieutenant-Governor, administered the state.
11 July 1933– 4 Oct 1948	Sir James Mitchell, GCMG, Lieutenant-Governor, administered the state.
5 Oct 1948– 30 June 1951	Sir James Mitchell, GCMG, Governor.
1 July 1951– 6 Aug 1951	Sir John Patrick Dwyer, KCMG, administered the state.
7 Aug 1951– 27 Aug 1951	Albert Asher Wolff administered the state.
28 Aug 1951– 5 Nov 1951	Sir John Patrick Dwyer, KCMG, administered the state.
6 Nov 1951– 26 June 1963	Lieutenant-General Sir Charles Henry Gairdner, KCMG, KCVO, KBE, CB, Governor.
26 June 1963– 25 Oct 1963	Sir John Patrick Dwyer, KCMG, Lieutenant-Governor, administered the state.
25 Oct 1963– 28 Aug 1973	Major-General Sir Douglas Anthony Kendrew, KCMG, CB, CBE, DSO, Governor.
28 Aug 1973– 7 Jan 1974	Sir Albert Asher Wolff, KCMG, Lieutenant-Governor, administered the state.
7 Jan 1974– 3 Apr 1975	Air Commodore Hughie (later Sir Hughie) Idwal Edwards, VC, CB, DSO, OBE, DFC, Governor.

GOVERNORS OF WESTERN AUSTRALIA continued

3 Apr 1975– 24 Nov 1975	Commodore James Maxwell Ramsay, CBE, DSC, Lieutenant-Governor, administered the state.
24 Nov 1975– 24 Nov 1980	Air Chief Marshal Sir Wallace Kyle, GCB, KCVO, CBE, DSO, DFC, KStJ, Governor.
25 Nov 1980– 25 Nov 1983	Rear Admiral Sir Richard Trowbridge, KCVO, KStJ, Governor.
26 Nov 1983– 1 July 1984	Francis Theodore Page Burt, KCMG, Lieutenant-Governor, administered the state.
2 July 1984–	Professor Gordon Reid, Governor.

GOVERNORS OF TASMANIA

16 Feb 1804– 24 Mar 1810	Colonel David Collins Lieutenant-Governor.
24 Mar 1810– 20 Feb 1812	Lieutenant Edward Lord and Captain John Murray, as commandants, administered the colony.
20 Feb 1812– 4 Feb 1813	Major Andrew Geils, as commandant, administered the colony.
4 Feb 1813– 9 Apr 1817	Colonel Thomas Davey, Lieutenant-Governor.
9 Apr 1817– 14 May 1824	Colonel William Sorell, Lieutenant-Governor.
14 May 1824– 30 Oct 1836	Colonel George Arthur, Lieutenant-Governor.
31 Oct 1836– 5 Jan 1837	Lieutenant-Colonel Kenneth Snodgrass administered the colony.
6 Jan 1837– 21 Aug 1843	Sir John Franklin, RN, KCH, Lieutenant-Governor.
21 Aug 1843– 13 Oct 1846	Sir John Eardley-Wilmot, Bt, Lieutenant-Governor.
13 Oct 1846– 25 Jan 1847	Charles Joseph La Trobe administered the colony.
26 Jan 1847– 8 Jan 1855	Sir William Thomas Dennison, Lieutenant-Governor.
8 Jan 1855– 10 Dec 1861	Sir Henry Edward Fox Young, CB, Governor-in-Chief.
11 Dec 1861– 16 June 1862	Colonel Thomas Gore Browne administered the colony.
16 June 1862– 30 Dec 1868	Colonel Thomas Gore Browne, CB, Governor.
30 Dec 1868– 15 Jan 1869	Lieutenant-Colonel W. C. Trevor administered the colony.
15 Jan 1869– 28 Nov 1874	Charles Du Cane, Governor and Commander-in-Chief.
30 Nov 1874– 13 Jan 1875	Sir Francis Smith administered the colony.
13 Jan 1875– 5 Apr 1880	Frederick Aloysius Weld, CMG, Governor.
6 Apr 1880– 21 Oct 1880	Sir Francis Smith administered the colony.

GOVERNORS OF TASMANIA continued

21 Oct 1880– 6 Dec 1881	Sir John Henry Lefroy administered the colony.
7 Dec 1881– 28 Oct 1886	Major Sir George Cumine Strahan, KCMG, Governor.
29 Oct 1886– 18 Nov 1886	Chief Justice W. R. Giblin administered the colony.
18 Nov 1886– 11 Mar 1887	Sir William Dobson administered the colony.
11 Mar 1887– 30 Nov 1892	Sir Robert George Crookshank Hamilton, KCB, Governor and Commander-in-Chief of Tasmania and its Dependencies.
30 Nov 1892– 8 Aug 1893	Sir William Dobson administered the colony.
8 Aug 1893– 14 Aug 1900	Viscount Gormanston (Jenico William Joseph Preston), KCMG, Governor and Commander-in-Chief.
14 Aug 1900– 8 Nov 1901	Sir John Dodds administered the state.
8 Nov 1901– 16 Apr 1904	Captain Sir Arthur Elibank Havelock, GCMG, GCIE, Governor in and over the State of Tasmania and its Dependencies.
16 Apr 1904– 28 Oct 1904	Sir John Dodds administered the state.
28 Oct 1904– 20 May 1909	Sir Gerald Strickland, KCMG, Governor.
21 May 1909– 29 Sept 1909	Sir John Dodds administered the state.
29 Sept 1909– 10 Mar 1913	Major-General Sir Harry Barron, KCMG, CVO, Governor.
10 Mar 1913– 4 June 1913	Sir John Dodds administered the state.
4 June 1913– 31 Mar 1917	The Rt Hon Sir William Grey Ellison-Macartney, KCMG, Governor.
31 Mar 1917– 6 July 1917	Sir Herbert Nicholls administered the state.
6 July 1917– 9 Feb 1920	Sir Francis Alexander Newdigate Newdegate, KCMG, Governor.
9 Feb 1920– 16 Apr 1920	Sir Herbert Nicholls administered the state.
16 Apr 1920– 27 Jan 1922	Sir William Lamond Allardyce, KCMG, Governor.
28 Jan 1922– 22 Dec 1924	Sir Herbert Nicholls and, during his illness, Mr Justice Ewing administered the state.
23 Dec 1924– 23 Dec 1930	Captain Sir James O'Grady, KCMG, OBE, Governor.
23 Dec 1930– 4 Aug 1933	Sir Herbert Nicholls administered the state.
4 Aug 1933– 4 Aug 1945	Sir Ernest Clark, GCMG, KCB, CBE, Governor.
4 Aug 1945– 24 Dec 1945	Sir John Morris administered the state.
24 Dec 1945– 8 May 1951	Sir Hugh Binney, KCB, DSO, Governor.

GOVERNORS OF TASMANIA continued

23 Aug 1951– 4 June 1958	The Rt Hon Sir Ronald Hibbert Cross, Bt, KCVO, Governor.
4 June 1958– 21 Oct 1959	Sir Stanley Charles Burbury administered the state.
21 Oct 1959– 25 Mar 1963	Lord Rowallan (Thomas Godfrey Polson Corbett), KT, KBE, MC, Governor.
26 Mar 1963– 24 Sept 1963	Sir Stanley Charles Burbury administered the state.
24 Sept 1963– 11 July 1968	Lieutenant-General Sir Charles Henry Gairdner, GBE, KCMG, KCVO, CB, Governor.
12 July 1968– 1 Dec 1968	Sir Stanley Charles Burbury administered the state.
2 Dec 1968– 1 Dec 1973	Lieutenant-General Sir Edric Montague Bastyan, KCMG, KCVO, KBE, CB, Governor.
30 Nov 1973– 4 Dec 1973	Mr Justice Green, Chief Justice, administered the state.
5 Dec 1973– 1 Oct 1982	Sir Stanley Charles Burbury, KCVO, KBE, KStJ, Governor.
1 Oct 1982– 8 May 1987	Sir James Plimsoll, AC, CBE, Governor.
8 May 1987– 19 Oct 1987	Sir Guy Green, KBE, administered the state.
19 Oct 1987–	His Excellency General Sir Phillip Bennett, AC, KBE, DSO, Governor.

PRIME MINISTERS OF AUSTRALIA

NO	PRIME MINISTER	PARTY	PERIOD OF OFFICE
1	Edmund Barton	Protectionist	1 Jan 1901– 24 Sept 1903
2	Alfred Deakin	Protectionist	24 Sept 1903–27 Apr 1904
3	J. C. Watson	Labor*	27 Apr 1904–17 Aug 1904
4	G. H. Reid	Free Trade/ Protectionist Coalition	18 Aug 1904– 5 July 1905
5	Alfred Deakin	Protectionist	5 July 1905–13 Nov 1908
6	Andrew Fisher	Labor	13 Nov 1908– 2 June 1909
7	Alfred Deakin	Fusion†	2 June 1909–28 Apr 1910
8	Andrew Fisher	Labor	29 Apr 1910– 24 June 1913
9	Joseph Cook	Liberal	24 June 1913–17 Sept 1914
10	Andrew Fisher	Labor	17 Sept 1914– 27 Oct 1915
11	W. M. Hughes	Labor	27 Oct 1915–14 Nov 1916
12	W. M. Hughes	National Labor	14 Nov 1916–17 Feb 1917
13	W. M. Hughes	Nationalist	17 Feb 1917– 10 Jan 1918
14	W. M. Hughes	Nationalist	10 Jan 1918– 9 Feb 1923

*Until 1918, when the name Australian Labor Party was adopted throughout Australia, the Labor Party (until 1906 spelt Labour) was variously named. For this reason Labor rather than ALP has been used here.

†The 'fusion' of Free Traders and ex-Protectionist Tariff Reformers, and of Deakin's Protectionist followers.

PRIME MINISTERS OF AUSTRALIA continued

15	S. M. Bruce	Nationalist–Country Coalition	9 Feb 1923–22 Oct 1929
16	J. H. Scullin	Labor	22 Oct 1929– 6 Jan 1932
17	J. A. Lyons	United Australia Party	6 Jan 1932– 7 Nov 1938
18	J. A. Lyons	UAP–Country Coalition	7 Nov 1938– 7 Apr 1939
19	Sir Earl Page	Country–UAP Coalition	7 Apr 1939–26 Apr 1939
20	R. G. Menzies	UAP	26 Apr 1939–14 Mar 1940
21	R. G. Menzies	UAP–Country Coalition	14 Mar 1940–28 Oct 1940
22	R. G. Menzies	UAP–Country Coalition	28 Oct 1940–29 Aug 1941
23	A. W. Fadden	Country–UAP Coalition	29 Aug 1941– 7 Oct 1941
24	J. Curtin	Labor	7 Oct 1941–21 Sept 1943
25	J. Curtin	Labor	21 Sept 1943– 6 July 1945
26	F. M. Forde	Labor	6 July 1945–13 July 1945
27	J. B. Chifley	Labor	13 July 1945– 1 Nov 1946
28	J. B. Chifley	Labor	1 Nov 1946–19 Dec 1949
29	R. G. Menzies	Liberal–Country Coalition	19 Dec 1949–11 May 1951
30	R. G. Menzies	Liberal–Country Coalition	11 May 1951–11 Jan 1956
31	R. G. Menzies	Liberal–Country Coalition	11 Jan 1956–10 Dec 1958
32	R. G. Menzies	Liberal–Country Coalition	10 Dec 1958–18 Dec 1963
33	Sir Robert Menzies	Liberal–Country Coalition	18 Dec 1963–26 Jan 1966
34	H. E. Holt	Liberal–Country Coalition	26 Jan 1966–14 Dec 1966
35	H. E. Holt	Liberal–Country Coalition	14 Dec 1966–19 Dec 1967
36	J. McEwen	Liberal–Country Coalition	19 Dec 1967–10 Jan 1968
37	J. G. Gorton	Liberal–Country Coalition	10 Jan 1968–28 Feb 1968
38	J. G. Gorton	Liberal–Country Coalition	28 Feb 1968–12 Nov 1969
39	J. G. Gorton	Liberal–Country Coalition	12 Nov 1969–10 Mar 1971
40	W. McMahon	Liberal–Country Coalition	10 Mar 1971– 5 Dec 1972
41	E. G. Whitlam	Labor	5 Dec 1972–19 Dec 1972
42	E. G. Whitlam	Labor	19 Dec 1972–11 Nov 1975
43	J. M. Fraser	Liberal–National Country	11 Nov 1975–22 Dec 1975

PRIME MINISTERS OF AUSTRALIA continued

44	J. M. Fraser	Liberal–National Country Coalition	22 Dec 1975–20 Dec 1977
45	J. M. Fraser	Liberal–National Country Coalition	20 Dec 1977– 3 Nov 1980
46	J. M. Fraser	Liberal–National Country Coalition	3 Nov 1980–11 Mar 1983
47	R. J. Hawke	Labor	11 Mar 1983– 1 Dec 1984
48	R. J. Hawke	Labor	1 Dec 1984–11 July 1987
49	R. J. Hawke	Labor	11 July 1987–

PREMIERS OF NEW SOUTH WALES

Since responsible government.

PREMIER	PARTY	APPOINTED	
S. A. Donaldson		6 June	1856
C. Cowper		26 Aug	1856
H. W. Parker		3 Oct	1856
C. Cowper		7 Sept	1857
W. Forster		27 Oct	1859
J. Robertson		9 Mar	1860
C. Cowper		10 Jan	1861
J. Martin		16 Oct	1863
C. Cowper		3 Feb	1865
J. Martin		22 Jan	1866
J. Robertson		27 Oct	1868
C. Cowper		13 Jan	1870
(Sir) J. Martin		16 Dec	1870
H. Parkes		14 May	1872
J. Robertson		9 Feb	1875
H. Parkes		22 Mar	1877
(Sir) J. Robertson		17 Aug	1877
J. S. Farnell		18 Dec	1877
(Sir) H. Parkes		21 Dec	1878
A. Stuart		5 Jan	1883
G. R. Dibbs		7 Oct	1885
(Sir) J. Robertson		22 Dec	1885
(Sir) P. A. Jennings		26 Feb	1886
(Sir) H. Parkes		20 Jan	1887
G. R. Dibbs		17 Jan	1889
(Sir) H. Parkes		8 Mar	1889
G. R. Dibbs		23 Oct	1891
G. H. Reid		3 Aug	1894
W. J. Lyne		14 Sept	1899
J. See	Progressive	28 Mar	1901
T. Waddell	Ministerialist	15 June	1904
J. H. Carruthers	Liberal Reform	29 Aug	1904
G. C. Wade	Liberal	2 Oct	1907
J. S. T. McGowen	Labor	21 Oct	1910
W. A. Holman	Labor	30 June	1913
	Nationalist	15 Nov	1916
J. Storey	Labor	12 Apr	1920
J. Dooley	Labor	10 Oct	1921
(Sir) G. W. Fuller	Nationalist	20 Dec	1921
J. T. Lang	Labor	17 June	1925

T. R. Bavin	Nationalist	18 Oct	1927
J. T. Lang	Labor	4 Nov	1930
B. S. B. Stevens	UAP	16 May	1932
A. Mair	UAP	5 Aug	1939
W. J. McKell	Labor	16 May	1941
J. McGirr	Labor	6 Feb	1947
J. J. Cahill	Labor	3 Apr	1952
R. J. Heffron	Labor	28 Oct	1959
J. B. Renshaw	Labor	30 Apr	1964
(Sir) R. W. Askin	Liberal	13 May	1965
T. L. Lewis	Liberal	3 Jan	1975
(Sir) E. A. Willis	Liberal	23 Jan	1976
N. K. Wran	Labor	14 May	1976
B. J. Unsworth	Labor	4 July	1986

PREMIERS OF VICTORIA

Since responsible government.

PREMIER	PARTY	APPOINTED	
W. C. Haines		28 Nov	1855
J. O'Shanassy		11 Mar	1857
W. C. Haines		29 Apr	1857
J. O'Shanassy		10 Mar	1858
W. Nicholson		27 Oct	1859
R. Heales		26 Nov	1860
J. O'Shanassy		14 Nov	1861
J. McCulloch		27 June	1863
C. Sladen		6 May	1868
J. McCulloch		11 July	1868
J. A. MacPherson		20 Sept	1869
J. McCulloch		9 Apr	1870
C. G. Duffy		19 June	1871
J. G. Francis		10 June	1872
G. B. Kerferd		31 July	1874
G. Berry		7 Aug	1875
(Sir) J. McCulloch		20 Oct	1875
G. Berry		21 May	1877
J. Service		5 Mar	1880
G. Berry		3 Aug	1880
(Sir) B. O'Loghlen		9 July	1881
J. Service		8 Mar	1883
D. Gillies	Conservative–Liberal Co	18 Feb	1886
J. Munro	National–Liberal	5 Nov	1890
W. Shiels	Liberal	16 Feb	1892
J. B. Patterson	Conservative	23 Jan	1893
G. Turner	Liberal	27 Sept	1894
A. Mclean	Liberal	5 Dec	1899
(Sir) G. Turner	Liberal	19 Nov	1900
A. J. Peacock	Liberal	12 Feb	1901
W. H. Irvine	Reform	10 June	1902
T. Bent	Reform	16 Feb	1904
J. Murray	Liberal	8 Jan	1909
W. A. Watt	Liberal	18 May	1912
G. A. Elmslie	Labour	9 Dec	1913
W. A. Watt	Liberal	22 Dec	1913
(Sir) A. J. Peacock	Liberal	18 June	1914
J. Bowser	National	29 Nov	1917
H. S. W. Lawson	National	21 Mar	1918

N. Lawson	Allan Ministry/ National Country Coalition 7 Sept 1923–	19 Mar	1924
N. Lawson	National 19 Mar–	28 Apr	1924
(Sir) A. J. Peacock	National	28 Apr	1924
G. M. Prendergast	Labor	18 July	1924
J. Allan	Country–National Co	18 Nov	1924
E. J. Hogan	Labor	20 May	1927
(Sir) W. M. McPherson	National	22 Nov	1928
E. J. Hogan	Labor	12 Dec	1929
(Sir) S. S. Argyle	UAP–Country Co	19 May	1932
A. A. Dunstan	Country	2 Apr	1935
J. Cain	Labor	14 Sept	1943
A. A. Dunstan	Country–UAP Co	18 Sept	1943
I. Macfarlan	Liberal	2 Oct	1945
J. Cain	Labor	21 Nov	1945
T. T. Holloway	Liberal–Country Co	20 Nov	1947
T. T. Holloway	Liberal	3 Dec	1948
J. G. B. McDonald	Country	27 June	1950
T. T. Hollway	Electoral Reform	27 Oct	1952
J. G. B. McDonald	Country	31 Oct	1952
J. Cain	Labor	17 Dec	1952
(Sir) H. E. Bolte	Liberal and Country	8 June	1955
R. J. Hamer	Liberal	23 Aug	1973
L. H. S. Thompson	Liberal	5 Aug	1981
J. Cain	Labor	8 Apr	1982

PREMIERS OF QUEENSLAND

Since responsible government.

PREMIER	PARTY	APPOINTED	
R. G. W. Herbert		10 Dec	1859
A. Macalister		1 Feb	1866
R. G. W. Herbert		20 July	1866
A. Macalister		7 Aug	1866
R. R. Mackenzie		15 Aug	1867
C. Lilley		25 Nov	1868
A. H. Palmer		3 May	1870
A. Macalister		8 Jan	1874
G. Thorn		5 June	1876
J. Douglas		8 Mar	1877
T. McIlwraith		21 Jan	1879
S. W. Griffith		13 Nov	1883
(Sir) T. McIlwraith		13 June	1888
B. D. Morehead		30 Nov	1888
(Sir) S. W. Griffith		12 Aug	1890
(Sir) T. McIlwraith		27 Mar	1893
H. M. Nelson		27 Oct	1893
T. J. Byrnes		13 Apr	1898
J. R. Dickson		1 Oct	1898
A. Dawson		1 Dec	1899
R. Philp		7 Dec	1899
A. Morgan		17 Sept	1903
W. Kidston		19 Jan	1906
R. Philp		19 Nov	1907
W. Kidston		18 Feb	1908

D. F. Denham	Liberal	7 Feb	1911
T. J. Ryan	Labor	1 June	1915
E. G. Theodore	Labor	22 Oct	1919
W. N. Gillies	Labor	26 Feb	1925
W. McCormack	Labor	22 Oct	1925
A. E. Moore	Labor	21 May	1929
W. Forgan Smith	Labor	17 June	1932
F. A. Cooper	Labor	16 Sept	1942
E. M. Hanlon	Labor	7 Mar	1946
V. C. Gair	Labor	17 Jan	1952
G. F. R. Nicklin	Country–Liberal	12 Aug	1957
J. C. A. Pizzey	Country–Liberal	17 Jan	1968
G. W. W. Chalk	Country–Liberal	1 Aug	1968
J. Bjelke-Petersen	Country–Liberal	8 Aug	1968

PREMIERS OF SOUTH AUSTRALIA

Since responsible government.

PREMIER	PARTY	APPOINTED	
B. T. Finniss		24 Oct	1856
J. Baker		21 Aug	1857
R. R. Torrens		1 Sept	1857
R. D. Hanson		30 Sept	1857
T. Reynolds		9 May	1860
G. M. Waterhouse		8 Oct	1861
F. S. Dutton		4 July	1863
H. Ayers		15 July	1863
A. Blyth		4 Aug	1864
F. S. Dutton		22 Mar	1865
H. Ayers		20 Sept	1865
J. Hart		23 Oct	1865
J. P. Boucaut		28 Mar	1866
H. Ayers		3 May	1867
J. Hart		24 Sept	1868
H. Ayers		13 Oct	1868
H. B. T. Strangways		3 Nov	1868
J. Hart		30 May	1870
A. Blyth		10 Nov	1871
(Sir) H. Ayers		22 Jan	1872
A. Blyth		22 July	1873
J. P. Boucaut		3 June	1875
J. Colton		6 June	1876
J. P. Boucaut		26 Oct	1877
W. Morgan		27 Sept	1878
J. C. Bray		24 June	1881
J. Colton		16 June	1884
J. W. Downer		16 June	1885
T. Playford		11 June	1887
J. A. Cockburn		27 June	1889
T. Playford		19 Aug	1890
F. W. Holder		21 June 1892	
(Sir) J. W. Downer		15 Oct	1892
C. C. Kingston	Liberal	16 June	1893
V. L. Solomon	Conservative	1 Dec	1899
F. W. Holder	Liberal	8 Dec	1899
J. G. Jenkins	Liberal; Liberal–Conservative	15 May	1901
R. Butler	Conservative	1 Mar	1905

T. Price	Labor–Liberal Coalition	26 July	1905
A. H. Peake	Liberal	5 June	1909
J. Verran	Labor	3 June	1910
A. H. Peake	Liberal	17 Feb	1912
C. Vaughan	Labor	3 Apr	1915
A. H. Peake	Liberal–National Co	14 Jul	1917
H. N. Barwell	Liberal	8 Apr	1920
J. Gunn	Labor	16 Apr	1924
L. L. Hill	Labor	28 Aug	1926
R. L. Butler	Liberal–Country Co	8 Apr	1927
L. L. Hill	Labor	17 Apr	1930
R. S. Richards	Labor	13 Feb	1933
R. L. Butler	Liberal Country League	18 Apr	1933
(Sir) T. Playford	Liberal Country League	5 Nov	1938
F. H. Walsh	Labor	10 Mar	1965
D. A. Dunstan	Labor	1 June	1867
R. S. Hall	Liberal–Country League	17 Apr	1968
D. A. Dunstan	Labor	2 June	1970
J. D. Corcoran	Labor	15 Feb	1979
D. O. Tonkin	Liberal	18 Sept	1979
J. C. Bannon	Labor	10 Nov	1982

PREMIERS OF WESTERN AUSTRALIA

Since responsible government.

PREMIER	PARTY	APPOINTED	
(Sir) J. Forrest		29 Dec	1890
G. Throssell		15 Feb	1901
G. Leake		27 May	1901
A. E. Morgans		21 Nov	1901
G. Leake		23 Dec	1901
(Sir) W. H. James		1 July	1902
H. Daglish	Labor	10 Aug	1904
(Sir) C. H. Rason	Liberal	25 Aug	1905
(Sir) N. J. Moore	Liberal	7 May	1906
F. Wilson	Liberal	16 Sept	1910
J. Scadden	Labor	7 Oct	1911
F. Wilson	Liberal	27 July	1916
(Sir) H. B. Lefroy	Liberal	28 June	1917
(Sir) H. P. Colebatch	Liberal	17 Apr	1919
(Sir) J. Mitchell	National and Country Party	17 May	1919
P. Collier	Labor	16 Apr	1924
(Sir) J. Mitchell	National and Country Party	24 Apr	1930
P. Collier	Labor	24 Apr	1933
J. C. Willcock	Labor	20 Aug	1936
F. J. S. Wise	Labor	31 July	1945
(Sir) D. R. McLarty	Liberal–Country League and Country Party	1 Apr	1947
A. R. G. Hawke	Labor	23 Feb	1953
(Sir) D. Brand	Liberal–Country League and Country Party	2 Apr	1959

J. T. Tonkin	Labor	3 Mar	1971
(Sir) C. W. M. Court	Liberal–National Country Party	8 Apr	1974
R. J. O'Connor	Liberal–National Country Party	25 Jan	1982
B. T. Burke	Labor	19 Feb	1983

PREMIERS OF TASMANIA

Since responsible government.

PREMIER	PARTY	APPOINTED	
W. T. N. Champ		1 Nov	1856
T. G. Gregson		26 Feb	1857
W. P. Weston		25 Apr	1857
F. Smith		12 May	1857
W. P. Weston		1 Nov	1860
T. D. Chapman		2 Aug	1861
J. Whyte		20 Jan	1863
(Sir) R. Dry		24 Nov	1866
J. M. Wilson		4 Aug	1869
F. M. Innes		4 Nov	1872
A. Kennerley		4 Aug	1873
T. Reibey		20 July	1876
P. O. Fysh		9 Aug	1877
W. R. Giblin		5 Mar	1878
W. L. Crowther		20 Dec	1878
W. R. Giblin		30 Oct	1879
A. Douglas		15 Aug	1884
J. W. Agnew		8 Mar	1886
P. O. Fysh	Liberal	29 Mar	1887
H. Dobson	Conservative	17 Aug	1892
(Sir) E. Braddon	Liberal	14 Apr	1894
N. E. Lewis	Conservative	12 Oct	1899
W. B. Propsting	Liberal–Democrat	9 Apr	1903
J. W. Evans	Liberal	11 July	1904
(Sir) N. E. Lewis	Liberal Fusion	19 June	1909
J. Earle	Labor	20 Oct	1909
(Sir) N. E. Lewis	Liberal	27 Oct	1909
A. E. Solomon	Liberal	14 June	1912
J. Earle	Labor	6 Apr	1914
(Sir) W. Lee	Liberal; Nationalist	15 Apr	1916
J. B. Hayes	Nationalist–Country Co	12 Aug	1922
(Sir) W. Lee	Nationalist	14 Aug	1923
J. A. Lyons	Labor	25 Oct	1923
J. C. McPhee	Nationalist	15 June	1928
(Sir) W. Lee	Nationalist	15 Mar	1934
A. G. Ogilvie	Labor	22 June	1934
E. Dwyer-Gray	Labor	11 Jun	1939
R. Cosgrove	Labor	18 Dec	1939
E. Brooker	Labor	18 Dec	1947
(Sir) R. Cosgrove	Labor	25 Feb	1948
E. E. Reece	Labor	26 Aug	1969
W. A. Bethune	Liberal	26 May	1969
E. E. Reece	Labor	3 May	1972
W. A. Neilson	Labor	31 Mar	1975
D. A. Lowe	Labor	1 Dec	1977
H. N. Holgate	Labor	11 Nov	1981
R. T. Gray	Liberal	26 May	1982

NORTHERN TERRITORY ADMINISTRATORS

Under South Australia

GOVERNMENT RESIDENT, ESCAPE CLIFFS	PERIOD OF OFFICE
B. T. Finniss	1864–88
J. T. Manton (acting)	1866–67

GOVERNMENT RESIDENT, PALMERSTON	
G. W. Goyder	1869–70
Dr. J. S. Millner (acting)	1870
Captain B. Douglas	1870–73
Dr. J. S. Millner (acting)	1873
G. B. Scott	1873–76
E. W. Price	1876–83
G. R. McMinn (acting)	1883–84
J. L. Parsons	1884–90
J. G. Knight	1890–92
C. J. Dashwood	1892–1905
C. E. Herbert	1905–10
S. J. Mitchell	1910

Under the Commonwealth

ADMINISTRATOR, DARWIN	
S. J. Mitchell (acting)	1911–12
J. A. Gilruth	1912–19
H. E. Carey (Director)	1919
M. S. C. Smith (acting)	1919–21
E. T. Leane (acting)	1921
F. C. Urquhart	1921–26
E. C. Playford (acting)	1926–27
R. H. Weddell (Govt Resident, North Australia	1927–31
C. A. Cawood (Govt Resident, Central Australia)	1927–29
V. G. Carrington (Govt Resident, Central Australia)	1929–31
R. H. Weddell (Administrator, Northern Territory	1931–37
C. L. A. Abbott	1937–46
L. H. A. Giles (acting)	1946
A. R. Driver	1946–51
F. J. S. Wise	1951–56
J. C. Archer	1956–61
R. B. Nott	1961–64
R. L. Dean	1964–70
F. C. Chaney	1970–73
T. A. O'Brien (acting)	1973
J. N. Nelson	1973–75
E. F. Dwyer (acting)	1975–76
J. A. England	1976–80
E. E. Johnston	1981

CHIEF MINISTERS OF THE NORTHERN TERRITORY

Since self-government

CHIEF MINISTER	APPOINTED
P. Everingham	1978
I. Tuxworth	1984
S. Hatton	1986

*This illustration by Michael Fitzjames accompanied a review
in the* Times on Sunday *of Thomas Keneally's book*
The Playmaker *(1987). The book is based on the play* The
recruiting officer *produced by Ralph Clark, lieutenant
and diarist aboard the* Friendship, *which sailed with the first
fleet to Botany Bay in 1787.*

COURTESY KIM ANDERSON

IV

INDEX

INDEX

I *To 1788* **II** *1838* **III** *1888* **IV** *1938* **V** *From 1939* **VI** *Historical atlas* **VII** *Events and places* **VIII** *Historical dictionary* **IX** *A guide to sources* **X** *Historical statistics* **XI** *The guide and index*

51

I *To 1788* **II** *1838* **III** *1888* **IV** *1938* **V** *From 1939* **VI** *Historical atlas* **VII** *Events and places* **VIII** *Historical dictionary* **IX** *A guide to sources* **X** *Historical statistics* **XI** *The guide and index*

52

I *To 1788* **II** *1838* **III** *1888* **IV** *1938* **V** *From 1939* **VI** *Historical atlas* **VII** *Events and places* **VIII** *Historical dictionary* **IX** *A guide to sources* **X** *Historical statistics* **XI** *The guide and index*

54

I To 1788 II 1838 III 1888 IV 1938 V From 1939 VI Historical atlas VII Events and places VIII Historical dictionary IX A guide to sources X Historical statistics XI The guide and index

58

I *To 1788* **II** *1838* **III** *1888* **IV** *1938* **V** *From 1939* **VI** *Historical atlas* **VII** *Events and places* **VIII** *Historical dictionary* **IX** *A guide to sources* **X** *Historical statistics* **XI** *The guide and index*

60

I *To 1788* **II** *1838* **III** *1888* **IV** *1938* **V** *From 1939* **VI** *Historical atlas* **VII** *Events and places* **VIII** *Historical dictionary* **IX** *A guide to sources* **X** *Historical statistics* **XI** *The guide and index*

63

I *To 1788* **II** *1838* **III** *1888* **IV** *1938* **V** *From 1939* **VI** *Historical atlas* **VII** *Events and places* **VIII** *Historical dictionary* **IX** *A guide to sources* **X** *Historical statistics* **XI** *The guide and index*

64

I *To 1788* **II** *1838* **III** *1888* **IV** *1938* **V** *From 1939* **VI** *Historical atlas* **VII** *Events and places* **VIII** *Historical dictionary* **IX** *A guide to sources* **X** *Historical statistics* **XI** *The guide and index*

66

I *To 1788* **II** *1838* **III** *1888* **IV** *1938* **V** *From 1939* **VI** *Historical atlas* **VII** *Events and places* **VIII** *Historical dictionary* **IX** *A guide to sources* **X** *Historical statistics* **XI** *The guide and index*

67

I *To 1788* **II** *1838* **III** *1888* **IV** *1938* **V** *From 1939* **VI** *Historical atlas* **VII** *Events and places* **VIII** *Historical dictionary* **IX** *A guide to sources* **X** *Historical statistics* **XI** *The guide and index*

I *To 1788* **II** *1838* **III** *1888* **IV** *1938* **V** *From 1939* **VI** *Historical atlas* **VII** *Events and places* **VIII** *Historical dictionary* **IX** *A guide to sources* **X** *Historical statistics* **XI** *The guide and index*

71

I *To 1788* **II** *1838* **III** *1888* **IV** *1938* **V** *From 1939* **VI** *Historical atlas* **VII** *Events and places* **VIII** *Historical dictionary* **IX** *A guide to sources* **X** *Historical statistics* **XI** *The guide and index*

72

I *To 1788* **II** *1838* **III** *1888* **IV** *1938* **V** *From 1939* **VI** *Historical atlas* **VII** *Events and places* **VIII** *Historical dictionary* **IX** *A guide to sources* **X** *Historical statistics* **XI** *The guide and index*

74

I To 1788 **II** 1838 **III** 1888 **IV** 1938 **V** From 1939 **VI** Historical atlas **VII** Events and places **VIII** Historical dictionary **IX** A guide to sources **X** Historical statistics **XI** The guide and index

76

I To 1788 **II** 1838 **III** 1888 **IV** 1938 **V** From 1939 **VI** Historical atlas **VII** Events and places **VIII** Historical dictionary **IX** A guide to sources **X** Historical statistics **XI** The guide and index

78

I *To 1788* **II** *1838* **III** *1888* **IV** *1938* **V** *From 1939* **VI** *Historical atlas* **VII** *Events and places* **VIII** *Historical dictionary* **IX** *A guide to sources* **X** *Historical statistics* **XI** *The guide and index*

79

I *To 1788* **II** *1838* **III** *1888* **IV** *1938* **V** *From 1939* **VI** *Historical atlas* **VII** *Events and places* **VIII** *Historical dictionary* **IX** *A guide to sources* **X** *Historical statistics* **XI** *The guide and index*

83